More Cruise Tips

with the Cruise Addict's Wife

Deb Graham

More Cruise Tips with the Cruise Addict's Wife

Deb Graham

Other Books by Deb Graham

Tips From The Cruise Addict's Wife

Mediterranean Cruise With The Cruise Addict's Wife

Peril In Paradise (a cruise novel)

How To Write Your Story

How To Complain ... and get what you deserve

Kid Food On A Stick

Quick and Clever Kids' Crafts

Awesome Science Experiments for Kids

Savory Mug Cooking

Uncommon Household Tips

4

Come Aboard!

Who doesn't want to cruise the open seas, save money, and have a better experience than anyone else on board? In this companion book to my *Tips From The Cruise Addict's Wife*, you'll learn even more tips to make the most of your cruise, whether it's your first or fifty-first. Wondering who to travel with, and how to get along if you're outvoted? I'm in favor of private tours; want to learn how to book the right ones, and save a boatload of money along the way? Which cruise line suits you, when's the best time to cruise, and how do you pick the right cabin? Wondering what to pack? What behavior will land you in the brig if you bring them? Did you know cruise ships have a brig? They do, and a morgue, too.

I hear I'm fun to travel with. Come along! You'll learn what to expect (and look out for) on your very first day on any ship.

The best way to cruise is to be the most informed person on any ship. It makes me crazy to see people save their money for an amazing once-in-a-lifetime cruise, then squander it on things they don't even value, simply because they don't know any better. It's as silly as conserving rainwater in a bucket while letting your bathtub run all weekend. Read on; I'm an expert on smart, frugal cruising, and I'm aiming to share my tips.

BONUS: At the end of this book, I include a chapter from *Mediterranean Cruise With The Cruise Addict's Wife*. Ever wondered about a cruise ship's grocery list, or how they can prepare 10,000 meals every single day? Don't miss it!

More Cruise Tips, which you hold in your hand, is a follow-up book to *Tips From The Cruise Addict's Wife*. Get it, if you haven't already read it! Often Number One on Amazon, it has hundreds of reviews, and it's selling like gangbusters. Thousands of people have read it, and told me it saved them money, and most importantly—made them the smartest passengers at sea. That makes me happy! If you're one of them, please leave me a review—I love reading them all.

The world's a vast and interesting place, and I want to see as much of it as I can while I'm here. My family, the women, especially, have wanderlust, what we call a Gypsy Gene. If any plan involves a suitcase, or better yet, a passport, count me in! I also have a fear of missing something wonderful, *right there*, when we travel. I firmly believe the best way to see a place is by being fully informed. Read, research, plan, then have a marvelous trip, doing exactly what you wish, secure in the knowledge that you're not missing a thing you care about.

The most important tip I can offer will change your whole cruise vacation: You Must Be The Most Informed Person On Any Ship. Well, leave the memorizing of charts and routes to those on the bridge, but for every other aspect of cruising, read all about it! Yes, I've met passengers who are surprisingly uninformed, but you don't want to be one of them.

By reading everything you can find about the ship, the cruise line, the itinerary, you're guaranteed to not miss a thing!

Why A Cruise Vacation?

You know those pioneers who crossed the plains, the gold-rush fortune seekers, the early sailors who cruised around the Horn in 1820? In any given day, you are bombarded with more data, more information, more input, then they received *in a year*. And the thousands of decisions we modern people make ...If you made a list, you'd be worn out before lunch, which you also have to think about. We live in a stressful time, and the need to hit the Reset Button is real.

A cruise might be just the thing! Cruising is growing every year in popularity, as cruise lines roll out bigger and fancier ships than ever before. It's hard to see the downside of waking up in a new place each day without the hassle of planning how to get there. And what a relief it is not to have to book hotels, find restaurants, and coordinate flights between cities. Cruising is definitely a vacation for the easygoing.

Do you want to learn to surf, play in a water park, go to a glitzy show every night? Is rock climbing your thing, or are you interested in lectures on photography, writing your personal history, entrepreneurship? Are you happiest reading a novel under a clear blue sky, or dancing until the wee hours in a glittery nightclub? Bask in the sun with a cheap novel, or take new cities by storm?

Want to vacation with four generations of your family, knowing that everyone from the toddler to Great Grandpa is happy and doing what they like best? Skydive, surf, roller skate, ride bumper cars, ice skate, golf, play basketball and volleyball? Try origami, line dancing, or a spinning class. A cruise is just the thing for an active traveler!

Are you a foodie? Grab a hot dog in the sunshine, enjoy paella by the pool, or dine in elegant five-star restaurants every night, with menus designed by well-known chefs. Is room service more your style?

Want to work out on state-of-the-art equipment, followed by a relaxing massage and sauna? You might enjoy a low-key class on flower arranging demo or a lecture on dabbling in the stock market. Working on your tan may be just what you need.

With cruising, much of the world is at your fingertips. Exploring a new place daily or enjoy leisurely sea days. Far from the city lights, Mother Nature puts on a show you just don't see at home. St Elmo's Fire skittering across the horizon or writhing Northern Lights from the top deck of a moving ship can't be beat. Have you ever seen a moonbeam dance on the ocean at night, or a sunset with a 180 degree view of the sky?

Want to see a show with an entertainer you really enjoy in an intimate venue, tickets included? You just might meet them around the ship. Maybe you'd like to go for long walks with the wind at your back as you walk around the ship. And I haven't even touched on romance. Cruise ship romance is legendary!

I warn you, cruising is addictive. We met a couple in March who said, "This is our ninth cruise since December." Others book back to back or longer cruises, combining itineraries that last for weeks–even months– on end. Nothing wrong with a weekend getaway, or a quick cruise down the coast.

I've met people who retired and *live* on a cruise ship. There must be something to it! A different cruise every week costs way less than the $4000- $6000 a month an assisted living place in North America costs, and a ship has all you need. Husband, alias The Cruise Addict, keeps dropping hints, suggesting this is how he'd like to live out his days.

One man told me after his wife died, all he wanted was someone to help with cooking and cleaning. An outgoing, energetic man, he craved having people around to talk to, and new things to do; no rocking chair in the corner for him! While he was remarkably healthy, it was a comfort having a doctor just a phone call away, no appointment needed. Somebody made up his bed every day, did his laundry, prepared his meals, took him to new and different places. Every week or so, 1800 new friends came onboard. His daughter in Omaha handled his mail and paid his bills, keeping him informed on family news by email and phone. At the end of this particular cruise, he was taking a week off from cruising to go meet the new great-grandchild and attend a granddaughter's recital. Smart man!

Cruises come in all shapes and sizes; read up, and you're bound to find the ones that suit you best. Mega-ships can feel more like a resort than a ship. Tall-masted sailing vessels put passengers to work hoisting sails and swabbing decks. That's the closest you're likely to come to being a pirate of the Caribbean. Most cruise ships fall between these extremes. Some cruise lines focus on enrichment courses, nature, history, and culture, while others strive to create a fun atmosphere rivalling Las Vegas or Disney. Itineraries can be port-intensive, visiting a different destination each day, or utterly relaxing, offering strings of lazy days at sea.

Ports can be familiar places, or exotic, ranging from sunny tropics to bustling cities to Antarctica, where zodiac boats take passengers to shore. Imagine swimming with penguins in a hot springs in the shadow of glaciers?

What's not to love?

Overcoming Objections

If you've ever mentioned cruising, I bet you've been met with one of two reactions. "Take me along!" or "Are you crazy?" followed by some objection. This is like taking the advice from the top authorities on child-raising; the ones who have never raised a child.

If you've read *Tips from a Cruise Addict's Wife*, you already know about our first cruise. Our anniversary was coming up, and I longed for an exotic vacation, somewhere romantic and interesting and special. I like being on the go. Lounging on a lovely, boring beach for days on end wasn't what I had in mind. I wanted to step off the world for little while, see new and different places without worrying about a long drive, flights, hotel arrangements, or planning entertainment.

Obviously, I wanted a cruise. Specifically, I wanted to go to Alaska, the last of the fifty US states I had yet to visit. Bonus– we live halfway between Seattle and Vancouver, BC, the two ports for Alaska cruises. No airfare or flights to wrangle.

Husband was, shall we say, *disinclined* to go. He was fairly clear in his objections, which I'll cover shortly. Story, first. He grumbled to his buddy, whose wife's uncle was a vice president of a major cruise line. He'd been encouraging her to cruise. Phone calls hastily made, dates finalized, and within half an hour, the four of us were booked on a dream Alaskan cruise!

Trapped, that's what he was. At least, that's the way Husband saw it. He griped, groused, complained, balked He verbally dug his heels in better than any old donkey, all the way to the port a few weeks later. Mercifully, he was silent as we four boarded the ship; three excited friends, one hangdog man planning to be abjectly miserable all week. Good thing he was quiet, because this was a vacation, not a kidnapping.

The ship's gleaming interior took our collective breath away. We dumped our bags in our staterooms, and set off to explore our home for the next eight days. Husband was only mildly interested, until we came into the forward-facing observation lounge on Deck Twelve. Canted glass on three sides, comfy chairs, a bar right there; full of potential! He liked the venue even better after sailaway, when the ever-changing scenery slipped by. For the rest of the cruise, any time we needed a meeting point, I knew where to find Husband; happily sitting in the very front chair, gazing out over the ocean and landscapes passing the floor-to-ceiling windows through the Inside Passage.

It took mere hours for Husband to morph into a molten puddle of relaxation, and to earn a new title: The Cruise Addict. Since then, he's been a poster boy for cruises. He's on every mailing list, he memorizes ship's names and gross tonnages, and if you mention a ship, he'll tell you where it sails. He's become skilled at finding The Best Deal ever. If we had a dollar for every cruise he's booked for friends and family, we could schedule another cruise tomorrow. Addicted, I tell you.

Let's get the common objections to cruising out of the way, shall we? I'll separate the valid ones from the less-so ones.

"Cruising Is Dangerous"

When I hear this objection, it's usually from people concerned about one of three things: bad weather, norovirus, and falling overboard. The exceptions are those who cruised on Navy ships to and from a war zone; their experience wasn't great. First of all, cruise ships are fast enough to be able to steer clear of large storms in all but rare cases, so that's not an issue. Second, there's about a 0.00001% chance of falling overboard. That number plummets even further if you don't get excessively drunk then attempt a tightrope walk on a ship's railing. Finally, less than one in one thousand sailings will have an outbreak of norovirus. And, even then, most of the passengers on the ship will remain unaffected.

If you're really worried about it, you probably shouldn't fly, let alone get in a car, because both are far more dangerous than taking a cruise. And be careful in the produce aisle; grapes are the number one hazard in grocery stores. Yes, really; you never see those little rugs in front of the corn chips display, do you?

"A Quick Port Day Is Not Enough Time To See Everything"

True. A day or two in a port isn't immersion. Renting an apartment for six months and getting to know the neighbors isn't the same as a cruise. I see cruises as a sort of sampler plate of a place, enabling me to decide which to return to later. I didn't love Turkey, but I could have happily taken root in Tuscany.

You're not going to see a huge city like Rome in a day, but you can't really see it in a couple of days, either. For that matter, there are places in your own hometown you haven't explored thoroughly. If there's just one destination you want to see, Omaha, for example, then a cruise probably isn't your best option. But for smaller ports in the Caribbean, a day in port is ample time to take an excursion, lie on the beach, and do some window shopping before heading back to the ship with time to spare. On a private tour, it's more than enough time to see the highlights. In some ports, including Maui and Venice, the ships park overnight, allowing plenty of time to wander.

You can't see it all. On the other hand, you'd be amazed at how much you *can* experience in a port, with a little advance planning. My philosophy is "I'd better see and do as much as I can; I may never get back to this wonderful place again." I like to book private tours –more about those later—with a local resident. They know the best places, what not to miss, and the shortcuts to avoid traffic and crowds. We've had some incredible experiences this way. Besides seeing a city through the eyes of someone who lives there, we've had some delightful surprises along the way. Recently unearthed archaeological digs, Changing of the Guard in three countries, enjoyed treats from a 220-year-old bakery; I've even been invited to olive-oil-pressing season at our driver's home in Greece. He insisted his mama made the best Greek pastries in the world.

It's a misconception among some self-appointed "worldly travelers" that cruises are a way to have fun in the sun, but not a good way to have an in-depth experience in a destination. You know who I mean, generally the kind who think watching TV is the same as visiting a city. They're wrong. You may tell them I said so.

"It Doesn't Go Anywhere"

Well, that's true of some cruises; some itineraries are under 150 miles, all told. Others circumnavigate the planet. Yes, you can go from Miami to the Bahamas and back, without really seeing much of anything. You can also book a 108-day around-the-world cruise that visits four continents and crosses the largest oceans in the world, plus the International Date Line, twice. You can book itineraries featuring ancient ruins and vibrant markets, historical castles and forts, breathtaking scenery, environmentally important areas, or the best beaches and tiki bars anywhere. It's completely up to you!

"I Don't Want To Be Stuck At Sea, So Far From Land, For Days On End"

Stepping off the world has its virtues, no doubt, but there's nothing wrong with keeping terra firma close at hand, as well. This is where choosing the right destination and itinerary makes all the difference. If you dream of long lazy days far away from your daily routine, a trans-oceanic repositioning cruise might be ideal for you. If you prefer keeping land nearby, try a Pacific Coastal itinerary, or a New England/Maritimes cruise. In the Caribbean, you can often see tomorrow's destination from today's pier. Port-intensive cruises let your feet touch land pretty much every day. Or, consider a good mix of both; many Hawaiian cruises leave from the mainland, with several sea days before reaching the islands.

"I'll Be Bored" ~OR~ "I Don't Want My Time Scheduled"

Personally, I think you'd have to work really hard to be bored on a cruise vacation. Sure, lazy sea days are less on-the-go than seeing a new port every day, but there's still plenty to do on a cruise ship. Relaxation is good for you; you're probably out of practice, like most North Americans. You can always bring a deck of cards or a dominoes set, a handicraft project you've been meaning to finish, and catch up on that reading you've put off. I freely admit I'm not very good at mindless relaxing. On a long cruise recently, I read eleven novels. That's eleven more than I read the previous year. Okay, I read fast, but *still-!*

Cruise Directors organize ship-board trivia tournaments, group games, sports competitions, classes, demos. Don't overlook the more tame activities, including watching the waves go by, admiring the horizon, looking for whales, dolphins, and flying fish, and striking up a conversation with another friendly cruiser. The cruising experience is what you make of it.

The beauty of cruising is that you control the type of day you have, from quiet to active. If you prefer to sleep in, then lounge the day away at the pool, you can. If working out, getting a facial, learning to line dance, taking a class on the stock market, and attending a Broadway-style performance is more your style, that's an option, too.

Choosing the right cruise line is important, and I'll get into that more in a bit. Besides the typical mainstream cruise ship offerings, you might consider a charter cruise with your specific interest in mind. Imagine days at sea with your favorite boy band, chef, or expert-in-their-field, whether that's oceanography, photography, or your favorite TV show. I'll talk more about themed cruises. For now, just know that if you have an interest, there's likely a cruise catering to it.

Evening activities include amazing entertainment options, such as ice bars, beach clubs, circus-style dinner theaters, Broadway shows, a large selection of funky bars and themed restaurants, dance parties, live music, and lots of karaoke. Don't forget port days, when what you choose to do is completely up to you. And I haven't even touched on the activities available for the kids!

"I'll Get Seasick"

Well, yes, you might, but you probably won't. And even if you do, there are a slew of remedies out there. Just because you turn green around the gills on a tiny fishing boat in choppy waters doesn't mean you'll suffer from mal de mer on a cruise ship. Modern ships have stabilizers, like wings, that can be extended under the waterline in rougher waters. They can calm the ship so even the worst storm feels well manageable. Of course, the itinerary makes a difference, as does the time of year. A North Atlantic cruise in November is more likely to hit some storms than a weekend jaunt from LA to Acapulco. The Mediterranean is often calmer than the Bering Sea. More on this coming up.

If you're the type who gets queasy looking at pictures of other people's cruises, you might consider a river cruise instead. Riverboats cruise the world's interior waterways, including Europe's Danube, Volga and Rhine Rivers, Egypt's Nile River, and China's Yangtze and Yellow Rivers. They're so port intensive, you'd be on land much of the time anyway, exploring by foot, motor coach or even bicycle. When you're onboard, you don't have to worry about waves or high seas that could make you sick. Personally, I'd try some of the remedies I'll recommend later before writing off "blue water" cruises.

"Cruises Are For Old People"

True, and young ones, and families, and singles, and theme-obsessed fans, and ... pretty much everyone in between. On our cruises, we've met a wide variety of passengers, including a couple dozen passengers in their nineties or older, even a WWI veteran. He could out-dance me every time, and the others took singular delight beating other teams in trivia. Age is a state of mind, you know!

Cruise ships and itineraries are designed with the whole family in mind. Many have amazing kids' clubs, and cater to the little ones wonderfully. Modern ships feature adult-only areas, where you can get away from noisy kids. Noisy adults–? Sorry, you're on your own.

All that said, some cruise lines do attract an older crowd, while others cater more to young families or singles. This is where carefully planning the right ship comes into play!

"I'll Get Claustrophobic Onboard"

This was Husband's biggest concern, along with the ship being overcrowded and boredom killing him off, outright. While onboard cabins tend to be smaller than the typical hotel room, they're laid out efficiently. Modern ships are like a floating hotel, with plenty of space. If you know you need more breathing room, spring for a balcony or a suite. On high-end luxury ships, suites can be as large as an average home, around 3000 square feet, with two bedrooms, two bathrooms, and a wrap-around balcony. Some also include a butler, which I bet you don't have at home.

Can't afford all that space? Don't worry. Some of the newest large ships are so big that first time cruisers sometimes forget they're on a ship. Designers put an emphasis on outdoor space, essentially carving out the middle of some ships to create an open-air midsection. If the stateroom walls feel like they are closing in on you, simply head toward the middle of the ship. Or push the elevator button with the highest number and – ta-DA! – all is well.

I know a woman who tends to claustrophobia, to the point where she doesn't even use try-on rooms when clothes shopping. When she cruises, she insists on a balcony, knowing an inside cabin, no matter how well laid-out, won't do at all. Watching for bargains, she can often book a balcony or suite for just a few bucks more than an inside cabin, or sometimes even less.

Even on a full sailing, the science and psychology put into ship design spreads passengers out so well, crowds are rare. Sure, there'll be a few hundred people exiting the theater after an evening show. Let the crowd disperse and you'll be fine. The one space I think you might feel claustrophobic on a ship is the shower. They're notoriously small, and some have shower curtains with a penchant for clinging to one's wet personal parts.

"Cruise Ships Aren't Real Ships, Not Like Actually Sailing"

Well, maybe. Some of the mega-ships turn activities inward, making the *ship* the focal point instead of the wide blue sea. Some newer cruise ships are more like floating hotels or resorts that just happen to visit a different place each day. Most ships have plenty of outdoor space, open decks, and wraparound promenades.

For those caught up in the allure of the open sea, choosing a ship will be critical. If you're yearning for a most authentic sailing experience, check out lines like Windstar, Star Clippers or Island Windjammers. They employ tall ships complete with masts and sails. The fairly no-frills accommodations and onboard amenities are offset by the thrill of sailing the open ocean like voyagers of old. If you ask, you can even help hoist the main sail! Instead of playing bingo or pool games, passengers can climb the ship's mast, lie out in the widow's net over the open sea, or stargaze at night. Water sports are a big emphasis on these cruises, with diving, snorkeling, and waterskiing trips organized by the ship's staff. A variety of water sports equipment (like snorkel gear and sea kayaks) is on hand for passenger use, free of charge.

"All That *Food*–! I Don't Want To Get Fat On A Cruise Ship!"

Cruise ships typically offer round-the-clock dining options, but no one is forcing you to pile on the food, or the pounds, either. In fact, I usually lose a few pounds on cruises, probably from all the extra walking we do as we explore new ports. As with anywhere else, you have total control over choices and portions. Is there ever any good reason to down a couple dozen bacon rashers at breakfast? Sure, you can eat both the prime rib and the lobster for dinner. You can order room service cheeseburgers at two in the morning. You can sample every creamy, gooey dessert offered. And you can do it the following day, too.

You can also sip green smoothies, enjoy heaping salads, broiled lean meats, and opt for fresh fruits for dessert. Every ship offers low-fat, gluten-free, and vegetarian options; it's up to you which you choose to eat. They're your lips, after all. Most cruise lines have traded in their midnight chocolate buffets for spa menus and sushi bars.

As a reminder; the gym is open 24 hours a day, and you're welcome to use it!

"I Can't Afford A Cruise"

I bet you can, if you're willing to shop around. Cruising is one of the most cost-effective vacations. It's not as cheap as pitching a tent in your backyard, but for the experience, you can't beat it. Cruise prices range from extremely cheap sale fares to sky-high prices on luxury lines. I've seen prices as low as $35 per person, per night to over $2000 per person per night for fancy suites on high-end cruise lines. Prices swing wildly, even on the same ship, depending on amenities, itinerary, time of year, and sailing capacity.

Consider what you get for the money. Cruises include 24 hour a day food service, live entertainment, lodging, most activities, access to state-of-the-art workout equipment, and nighttime entertainment. And I didn't mention transportation from port to port and dedicated children's programs. I will, soon.

When you factor in all you'd spend on a similar land vacation, you'll be amazed to see how much less a cruise can cost. Let's look at Hawaii. Norwegian Cruise Line visits five ports in a seven day cruise, two of them overnight ports, starting at around $999 per person. For you to *fly* to each of those cities, book a hotel in each place and buy meals would cost several times that much, before you add in entertainment. Plus, you'd miss all the fun onboard activities and shows, plus the joy of watching the ocean sail by.

"I'm Not Going To Like It, I Just Know It"

In all of our cruises, I have met less than a dozen people who dislike cruising, not including those stick-in-the-mud types who won't give it a try. My own sister says cruising is "not my cup of tea". On the other hand, her idea of tea is literally a pot of tea with strangers at midnight in a souk in Iran. She's not your standard tourist! A friend of mine is a photographer and a bird watcher. His style of travel is to plant himself in one spot before dawn, not moving until late afternoon, photographing anything feathery that flies by. That's not really feasible on a cruise. He'd be better off taking a long weekend to some wilderness locale.

If you're an ordinary adventure seeker, give cruising a try!

Travel Agent, Or Book Your Own?

I'm a writer – you may have noticed – and this question is similar to the ongoing question among authors: Should I self-publish, or hope a publishing house will count me worthy? Surprisingly, the answer is the same as the travel agent question. "What can they do for me that I can't do for myself, easier and faster?" It's all about advantages, disadvantages, and how much control do you want over your own project/vacation/next Great American Novel.

When an author opts for a traditional publishing house, they're at their mercy. Once that contract is signed, it's out of the author's hands. I've seen covers, character names, scenes, themes, even genres, changed in ways the writer never intended. In the Olden Days – say, fifteen years ago – publishers handled marketing, publicity, and distribution. Or else they didn't, leaving you with five thousand copies of an unsold book in your garage. I know authors who still lean heavily on publishers. They admit they are making less money, have less control over their work, and are perfectly capable of accessing any resource the traditional publishing houses have, including cover design, marketing, editing and all. The honest ones admit they're afraid.

I look at travel agents the same way. Once you book through a travel agent, you can no longer discuss *anything* regarding your upcoming cruises directly with the cruise line. On the one hand, it's nice to have a middleman to run interference for you. On the other hand, it's also nice to be able to speak to the cruise line representative twenty-four hours a day, regardless of whether or not it's your agent's day off, or it's 3 a.m. and that thought just occurred to you when your agent may not be available.

On the other hand, it's fun to keep a watch on prices of your booked cruise as the day draws near. They can swing wildly, and if you act fast, you can easily save hundreds of dollars on a booking. On the other hand, it's good to have a sharp agent to keep watch *for* you. On the other hand, you're not their only client; do you trust them to be as concerned as *you* are about your trip? You can easily set up a "watch" on a website to notify you of price changes. If the prices lowers, you can make the call; if it goes up, you can gloat about how smart you were to book when you did.

With the same technology literally at your fingertips, booking your own cruise is easy. Nothing is stopping you from comparing itineraries, cabins, ship amenities, and all, utilizing the exact same websites a travel agent uses. On the other hand, a knowledgeable agent can point out things you might overlook. An adjoining cabin has only a chair, not a couch, the mosquitoes that month are as big as mini cupcakes, or a parallel itinerary stops at two more ports than the one you had in mind. On the other hand, you're perfectly capable of learning all that yourself. On the other hand, will you take the time to do so?

As you can see, this question raises enough Other Hands to build a fine octopus. In the end, which is better for *you*?

With a non-complicated cruise itinerary, you're perfectly capable of tracking down a good price, reading up on which cabin suits you, and booking the cruise through the cruise line itself or a third-party site online. If it's matter of driving to the port, and getting onboard, you're fine. If you're taking four flights to the port, and booking complicated triple back-to-back cruises on three different lines, or you just aren't confident, you might be better off seeking help with logistics.

A good travel agent (keyword: *good*) will check for price drops for you and automatically get you the lower price. Not all travel agents will do this. You'd better ask any potential travel agent if this is part of their services. I've heard of agents charging $65 per phone call, and an additional $25 if they change the booking to get the lower price. In other words, the price drop would have to be significant, to make it worthwhile. In my so-who-asked opinion: find a better travel agent, one who has your best interest in mind!

A common myth is that using a travel agent will cost you more than booking it yourself. In reality, the opposite can be true. Some travel agents charge for booking, changes, and all follow up phone calls. In my opinion, these are not for you; let the less-knowledgeable people make up their clientele. Respectable travel agents can save money, and offer good advice.

Travel agents often pass along group rates, and savings. They buy out blocks of cabins on cruises, then offer the group rate to their clients, not available to the general public. We've done these several times. On one cruise, we were part of a group of 268 passengers, and never identified a one of them. Added amenities are often part-and-parcel, such as onboard credit, free photos, a bottle of wine, in-room treats, and complimentary dinners at specialty restaurants.

Travel agents receive emails daily from the cruise lines informing them of special promotions, then they pass this information along to their customers. By using an agent, you can take advantage of these promotions that you may have otherwise never have known about. Back to that octopus ... you can easily get these same mailings.

What do *I* do? Husband and I have used the services of a travel agent intermittently. Our trusted travel agent died last year, at the age of much-too-young. He was great. He'd often find deals we'd missed, recommend extras like hotel-and-transfer packages cheaper than we could book on our own, and he made helpful suggestions. He was honest enough to tell us when we found a better price than he could offer. We miss him.

Husband's alias is The Cruise Addict, and he's on every cruise line's preferred mailing list. They send him specials and deals that few ever see. We know enough to book all but the most complicated voyages on our own. Your mileage may vary, and that's okay with me.

You might keep this in mind: Cruise lines want to sail with a full ship. As sailing date nears, they will call booked passengers, offering upgrades for free or very cheap prices–think $12 a day for a suite over the inside cabin you booked, or a free balcony upgrade. Cruise lines deny bias, but they seem to prefer to hand out upgrades without a middleman involved in the conversation. In my own experience, and the anecdotal research I've done, *no one* who's had a significant upgrade ever used a travel agent to book that cruise! If you're looking for ways to lure the Upgrade Fairy, this could be the fact that tips the scales for you. On the other hand, we all know fairies are elusive creatures.

When Is The Best Time To Cruise?

Hurray for vacation time! A chance to step off the world and out of your routine, experience new places and see new things, meet interesting people, maybe even learn some history or culture along the way, is too precious to waste!

Of course, the best time to go is when you *can* go. If you teach high school, you'll be limited by the school schedule. If you have a baby, you'll have to wait until Cutie Pie is over six months old; likewise, if you're more than five months pregnant, you can't cruise. Two weeks after you start a new job may not be the best for that three-month cruise. Do you need to schedule around school breaks – or want to avoid hordes of joyful children? Is a holiday week the best time for your cruise? Is your main goal to escape frigid winter temperatures at home?

Keep in mind the fact that cruises always seek the best weather. Many itineraries are not available year-round. You simply can't do a Scandinavian cruise in January, or cruise Alaska in February. With some exceptions, cruise ships move around to different regions throughout the year, a few months in each place. These one-way repositioning cruises can be a bargain, as well as a taste of both itineraries. A trans-Atlantic cruise from Miami to Stockholm gives you a few tropical days, then the temperatures dip a few degrees each day, concluding with where's-my-jacket weather.

And, of course, the timing matters, even within the season. Fall foliage enthusiasts, for instance, will find September and October the best time to take that Canada/New

England cruise, keeping in mind the peak of "the colors" varies every year.

Water-sports lovers and families tend to prefer warm regions in the summer, when school is out and temperatures are warm enough for swimming. Personally, if the ocean is chillier than bathwater, I'm happier staying on the beach. Why is it children can't seem to feel cold temperatures? I've seen our young grandsons with blue lips, screaming, "I'm not cold!" as a parent hauls them out to dry.

The best time to cruise to Alaska is influenced by your preferences for viewing wildlife, fishing, bargain-shopping, the best time for avoiding blizzards, and when the Northern Lights are most active. You may run into a dusting of snow in May, a heat wave in July. That's relative—it's still Alaska! There's less chance of rain in May and August, and the best shopping bargains occur in September.

For most cruise itineraries, there are periods of peak demand (high season), moderate demand (shoulder season), and low demand (low season). Low and shoulder seasons yield the most bargain opportunities in year-round destinations. In places that have a longer sailing season, such as Bermuda, the low season is a few weeks after cruises begin and before they end. For Panama Canal and Northern European cruises, almost all sailings are priced "in season," and bargains are hard to come by. We've found them; you just have to look a little harder.

Shoulder-season cruises often have less-than-full sailings, smaller crowds, and cheaper prices as a result of the weather gamble. The humidity may be killer, it might snow in the North, or the ship might miss a port while dodging a hurricane. Or, more likely, you'll have a delightful, uneventful trip for 40% less than last month's cost.

Cruises will be most crowded over the summer months and holidays, when kids are out of school. And who can resist the ease of a family reunion at sea?

Prices often fluctuate based on kids' availability. Spring break, for example, is a popular (and pricey) time of year, but the last week in August, when most children return to school, is a bargain. The first couple weeks of the year tend to be low priced, as most people catch their breath from the holiday flurry. That's when our wedding anniversary falls. By the time I make it through Thanksgiving, Christmas, and New Year's, I'm too tired to celebrate.

If you'd rather not be surrounded by kids, avoid summer and holiday cruises, when fully a third of passengers can be children. Longer cruises tend to attract older, retired passengers; working folks can't afford that much time off. You know what Shakespeare said about "Know thyself"? It applies to cruising, too. What's most important to you?

Three-night cruises to warm-weather destinations like Mexico, Bermuda, and the Caribbean tend to attract twenty-somethings looking for a party.

Short cruises in Europe and Asia won't have the same wild vibe. Americans know how to party. I was concerned as we boarded a three-day Pacific Coastal cruise. The group of college-aged people in front of us wore matching shirts announcing, "Jamie's Bachelor Bash." Not a good omen! Turned out the group of fifteen guys were there to have good clean fun, not rabble-rouse. They were first in every activity, won the cannonball splash, and lit up the karaoke night. Their enthusiasm was contagious. It could have been a lot worse!

Choosing an Itinerary

Alice: Would you tell me, please, which way I ought to go from here?
The Cheshire Cat: That depends a good deal on where you want to get to.
Alice: I don't much care where ...
The Cheshire Cat: Then it doesn't much matter which way you go.
Alice: ... So long as I get somewhere.
The Cheshire Cat: Oh, you're sure to do that, if only you walk long enough.

— **Lewis Carroll**   *Alice in Wonderland*

Are you into relaxing? Partying? Cultural experiences? Family time? Environmental exploration? Do you want to be on the go, on the stage, or on the beach? If you haven't thought through where you want to go, you're not likely to get there.

Some cruise lines specialize in immersion cruises. They focus on local cuisine and entertainment, with classes onboard covering history, geography, social aspects, resume-fodder skills, and more. And of course, once in port, you're not tied to any regimented plan. Even standard mainstream cruises to seemingly civilized locales allow for plenty of adventure. Rent a jeep, go off-roading, connect with a local, try spelunking, book a private tour, sit in a café people-watching, go rock climbing, window shop until you find the very item your heart desires, even if you didn't know it existed until you laid eyes on it.

A few smaller cruise lines focus on adventure and enrichment. Remote destinations like Antarctica, the Arctic, around Cape Horn, to the Galapagos and other off-the-beaten-path destinations suddenly become possibilities. Longing to swim with penguins in the wild? See Norway's fjords, watch spawning salmon fighting their way upstream, linger above the Arctic Circle? Some lines partner with National Geographic or The Travel Channel. Each voyage boasts scientists, naturalists, oceanographers, and photographers onboard to ensure adventurous passengers capture great memories to take back home. These smaller ships carry under 200 passengers, allowing an in-depth, "up close and personal" adventure.

It's your vacation!

Cruise lines are in heated competition for a bigger share of the cruising market. To that end, ships are constantly adding new and different onboard experiences. Passengers can rock climb, play miniature golf, learn to surf, ride a carousel or bumper cars, tackle ropes courses, enjoy a spa treatment, work out in a full-size gym, lie by a "beach" pool or in a hot tub, ride a zip line, ice skate, all right onboard.

Ships feature a different variety of live entertainment every night, including comedy shows, Broadway-type musicals, parades and acrobatic shows. You can improve your tennis game, work the stock market, learn to scuba dive, take a photography class, practice cake decorating, take in a sushi or pasta-making class, watch the big game in a sports bar, and dance with a live DJ, all before Day Three, if you choose.

Keep in mind, the large mega-ships cannot go to some of the off-the-beaten-track villages or islands. Their infrastructure just can't accommodate an extra few thousand people, even for a day. Even if the ship can tender passengers into a smaller port, the tendering time would take away from your time ashore. If that's what you're after, you're going to have to consider smaller ships. Lucky for you, cruising has nearly endless options!

On the other hand, many marvelous islands in the Caribbean are set up to accommodate ships of all sizes. Most major sea coast cities in the world have cruise ship docks, allowing large ships to dock easily.

Where to Cruise?

I speak fast, I think fast, I decide fast. However, I take pride in being carefully non-committal when somebody else needs to make the decision. When our adult kids come to me for advice, I'll pelt them with options, suggest they make a pro/con chart, and help them see all possibilities, but I refuse to say, "Just get the blue one, already!"

I won't tell you where to cruise, either, at least not outright. Just for comparison's sake, let's look at some regions.

Alaska

Okay, disregard the previous paragraph. If you have the chance to visit Alaska, **GO**. I've toured all fifty US states, and over 30 countries. Alaska cast a spell over me like no other place I've visited! The scenery, the people, the sense of vast potential, the very *air*, affected me in a way I can't describe. Forget San Francisco; I left a part of my heart in Alaska. I've been on a handful of cruises to Alaska, and I tell you, I'd go again tomorrow if I could. After all, I need to go visit my left-behind body part.

Alaska's High Season runs June through August. Ships sail May through September, with cruise lines pushing both ends a week or so longer most years. With Alaska being so popular, super-cheap deals are unlikely, but it's worth it! There are places in Alaska you can only see by cruise ship, including Glacier Bay. Sure, you could fly in and puddle-jump around the state, but you can only see the glacier faces from the sea.

I'm a big fan of glaciers. Did you know they speak? Native American and First Nation peoples believe glaciers are alive. Sure, mock, from your city recliner. Standing right there, hearing the glaciers creak and groan under centuries of moving ice, their very spirits permeating the air as ranch-house sized calves break free ...   I'm convinced. Of course, they're alive.

I know you picture those old movies where the sourdoughs slog through waist-high snow with their beards frozen to their chests. That happens ... but not during cruise season, and not along the southern coast, where cruise ships go. Alaska's temperatures are at their warmest in July and August, taking into account Mother Nature's attitude; this can vary wildly day to day. You may encounter 80 degrees one day and sideways sleet the next. The later into summer you go, the better your chances of seeing wildlife, after hibernation is good and over. Babies of all species are abundant in early summer. And *adorable*–have you ever seen a baby porcupine or otter? Makes you want to scoop one up to cuddle ... if not for the fact that their mom would rip your face off, none too gently.

Alaska is known for wilderness, and a couple of miles out of any town, there's plenty of that. But keep in mind, with so many ships sailing Alaska now, there can be serious congestion in small-town ports. I'm not a fan of elbow to elbow crowds, even on historic boardwalks. The way around this: book a private or ship's tour to get off the main drag. Renting a car is a wonderful idea in Skagway, where you can drive up into the Yukon, but not as feasible elsewhere. Alaska has less connecting roads than the rest of the country. Even in Juneau, the capital city, the road ends about eight miles out of town. It's also one of only two American capitals unreachable by road. Guess the other? Honolulu!

Sailing in the early or late shoulder season has advantages, beyond lower prices. You're more likely to see the Northern Lights in later summer, and the snow-capped mountains are at their prettiest in early summer. They're gorgeous when they are in summer-melt-mode, too, but all those white glistening snow and the waterfalls cascading every few feet...Aaahhh.

As winter approaches, stores are eager to move their merchandise before they roll up the sidewalks for the winter. A person can tie up Christmas shopping early, while saving a bundle. Surely your youngest family members need a fuzzy moose hand puppet, 90% off, right?

Risks include excursions being cancelled if winter gives one last gasp, especially tours involving helicopters. You might be enchanted to wake up to find snow on your balcony, but bear in mind, Denali National Park has been known to close as early as September if the white fluff piles up.

Australia

High Season: Late November to March. Shoulder Season: May through September

Who doesn't want to visit Oz? Remember your grade-school geography? Australia is both the largest island and the smallest continent in the world. A big advantage for sun-seekers: when it's winter in North America, it's summer in Australia. You can expect nearly perfect weather in the large ports of call of Sydney, Adelaide, and Perth, with sub-tropical climate in the northeast Queensland region. High cruise season is also typhoon season, leading to occasional rough sailings. Aussies often vacation between late December and late January, so expect big crowds and jammed ports during that time. In the low season, weather extremes are unlikely, and crowds in ports are less.

At any time of the year, on public transport and any place more than one Australian is gathered, you're likely to hear this odd chant break out:

"Aussie, Aussie, Aussie!"

by one or more people, out of the blue, met by shouts of

"Oi, Oi, Oi!!"

for no good reason at all. It's a common cheer at Australian sport events, and it's spreading. Since the 2000 Olympics, I've heard it hollered on ships, including across the formal dining room, in line to board the ship, and once during the introduction of an *American* performer on stage.

A man in the audience stood and screamed "Aussie, Aussie, Aussie!"

With no hesitation, the whole ship's band stood and shouted *"Oi, Oi, Oi!"* as if they'd rehearsed.

Once that was out of their systems, the show went on. One of the best reasons to travel; they're not like the people in your hometown, and that's a good thing.

Canada/New England

One of the main reasons folks book cruises to New England and the Canadian Maritimes is for the scenery, notably, the fall foliage. Trouble is, it's hard to predict when leaves will turn colors, months in advance. We've lucked out every time, but others a week one way or the other missed out. Seeing green leaves "about to turn" looks a lot like any midsummer tree. With so much history running through this itinerary, go anyway. If your gamble pays off with regard to brilliant leaf-colors, count it a big bonus!

Canada/New England's season runs from May to October. Temperatures can be chilly late in the season, the farther north you go. That can be a benefit, since these ports are ideal for long walks andcasual strolls. Mid-summer's oppressively humid, hot days are less than wonderful, if you're not from the area. If you *are* from the Mid-Atlantic, you're used to it. Like us Seattle-ites, who endure near-daily drizzle nine months out of the year, just sigh and go on. Other than middle of August, bring a light jacket. Problem solved.

Once most kids are back in school in September, the ships tend to be a little quieter. Halifax, Boston and St. Johns are not known for being party towns; that crowd aims for warm climates and sandy beaches. Overall, we've found the friendliest people in the world in the small Canadian towns along this route. They go all out, welcoming cruise ships, complete with marching bands, mayor in full regalia, and RCMP there, just for posing in photos. Wait; was that Nanaimo, on Canada's Western coast? Either way, small towns go all out to welcome cruisers (and their money).

The Caribbean

The Caribbean has the longest sailing season anywhere, making cheap cruises easy to find most of the year. The high season tends to be late June through August, and Christmas/ New Year's, and February to mid-April. Did you track that? That's school's summer vacation, holiday break, and Spring Break (mostly for college kids who can afford a cheap cruise, or wheedle their parents into it). During peak weeks, prices can be significantly higher.

Mid winter, especially around Christmas, is when the poor half-frozen Northerners declare, "That's it, we're outta here!" and plan a warm-weather cruise. Did you also know that Florida's real estate market booms during a severe winter, with Michiganders and others realizing they don't have to live like that?

Cruising during the school holidays can be a great time to sail with kids. Children's programs are in full swing, even on lines that don't typically cater to them. Plus, it's easier for children to make friends onboard, unlike that Mediterranean cruise we took that had a total of two –count 'em, *two* – children onboard, not counting the adorable 18-month old twins.

People looking for peace and quiet will want to avoid peak weeks like the plague, as ships are at their highest capacity. If you just want to read a book, overcrowded ports and noisy ships overrun with rowdy kids and teens and half-drunk spring-breakers is *not* your best option.

Off-season times for the Caribbean include late April through May (once most colleges get past spring break), and September to early January (excluding holiday weeks). Of course, a good chunk of that calendar covers hurricane season. That's June-November, as if Mother Nature reads calendars. If a storm brews around Florida or the Caribbean, the cruise might change ports of call. Even with diversions, you still might experience rain and rough seas these weeks.

On the other hand, we've missed ports quite often for un-weather-related causes, and life goes on. Cruise lines take safety seriously. No captain worth his salt is going to sail into a storm, against the National Weather Service's advisories. Oh, that episode with the *Serenade of the Seas?* Don't think about it.

The first port we ever missed was in the Caribbean. The Captain apologized and offered free rum punch. I was playing Ping-Pong with my fifteen-year-old son when the announcement was broadcast.

I asked "Want some rum punch?" His eyes lit up: Mom had lost her mind, right in front of him. As he nodded eagerly, I asked a nearby bar waiter for, "Two rum punch, please, with no rum." Son's shoulders sagged. Mom was still on duty.

Oddly, the next two times we missed a port were on different ships, different itineraries, but with the same Captain, and the same apology, same rum punch offer. Oh, by the way, don't worry about missing a port if you have a tour scheduled. If it's through the cruise line, they automatically refund your money. If you booked a private tour, just call them as soon as you can to tell them you won't be showing up. In every case I've ever heard of, they refund your deposit in a heartbeat. Local tour companies monitor the ships closely. Chances are, they'll know you're going to miss that port before you do!

The biggest benefit of taking this infinitesimal chance on a rare hurricane hitting your exact dot on the globe at that precise week are the great deals you can score. It's common to find cruises for hundreds of dollars less than the same cruise at peak times. Autumn, especially, tends to be a good time to snag bargains. I've seen many cruises for under $35 a day, per person, which is less than dining out at a decent place.

European River/Canal Cruises

I admit I haven't been on a "green water' cruise, for several reasons. First, I'm cheap, and they are not. I love the ocean—there's something primeval about watching the wake of a cruise ship, or the waves against the side of a sea-going vessel. While river boats' top cruising speed is around two miles per hour, that's not even enough to ruffle my hair!

However, I hear river cruises are lovely, and they certainly have a following. These routes are not on typical big cruise ships, but more of a flotilla of low-keel river boats and cruise barges. Their itineraries follow Europe's main rivers like lace on a map, and are quite port-intensive. Springtime flowers make April and May popular times to go, but beware the annual spring flooding from the annual spring heavy rains that causes problems ... well, annually. In at least a few places every year, the rivers swell, making bridges too low and locks unusable for river boats' passage.

Conversely, summer temperatures can cause the rivers' level to drop very low, making it impossible for boats to move. When this happens, passengers are taken to the various cities by motor coach; in effect, a really expensive bus tour. And don't expect to see as many – if any – kids there as you do on the bigger ships, even during the summer. These much smaller cruises cater to an adult clientele.

While tamer than "blue water" cruises, there's plenty to explore at a leisurely pace. Itineraries include visits to wine countries, historic city centers, Christmas markets, ancient tombs, old cities, castles, and cathedrals, all while beautiful countryside vistas glide past your window at a mild pace.

Ocean-going cruise lines sail their ships year round, moving them from place to place, depending on the season. European river and canal ships operate seasonally, mooring in January and February. If you're interested in the castles, cathedrals and quaint shops along the rivers without the summer crowds, aim for March and April.

Although the weather can be bitter, river cruises' popular Christmas Market cruises in November and December to Germany, Austria and Eastern Europe offer a unique way to dive into the charming seasonal shops along the route. You know that one-of-a-kind wood-and-eggshell Nativity scene you've dreamed of? If it exists, it's probably here.

While undeniably pricy, river cruises often boast two-for-one prices, or airfare- included deals.

Northern Europe

High season is June through September. Northern Europe is at its loveliest during the summer months, with ports that line the Baltic Sea and Norway's fjords in full feather. Temperatures are balmy, occasionally steamy, skies are generally sunny, and the cities turn themselves inside out after a long winter. Life is lived out of doors, whether it's getting out on the water or sipping beers at sidewalk cafes. On the flipside, summer cruises to the Baltic are often among the most expensive European cruises out there.

Low/Shoulder Season includes May and September, and don't write this period off. Kids are back in school, ports are quieter, places you long to see less crowded. The weather, whether spring-like or autumnal, is beautiful. Well, that's relative, as we all know.

We were in Stockholm in September. I found dusk's temperatures of low 40's brisk, yet residents spilled out of tiny restaurants, happily celebrating the last days of summer. Every restaurant provided a heap of fleece blankets for their customers, each a different color; red-wrapped diners there, orange ones across the way. I admit Husband and I took refuge inside an eatery. We were the only ones indoors. I guess knowing the long dark winter days were soon approaching made soaking up every last glimmer of warmth mandatory.

"Warmth" is also relative.

While temperatures may be a bit brisk in spring and fall, advantages abound. You'll avoid summer crowds, and cruise fares tend to be lower. Plus, those sunsets! In the USA, I've seen a whole lot of sunsets, including some breathtaking ones that looked like the whole horizon was on fire. Without variance, in America, the sun sets lower in the sky, then – plop– it drops behind the horizon. Not in Scandinavia. There, the sun leisurely circled the sky in a lazy arc, lowering a scant degree at a time, finally settling behind the sea, fully six hours after dusk began! That's my kind of sunset.

A couple of hardy cruise lines, smaller ones, offer mid-winter Scandinavian cruises. I don't know why. They tout the spectacular northern lights on display, but keep in mind that bitter cold and snow can obscure the scenery. If you're going to be forced inside much of the time ... Well, it's up to you.

Hawaii

A cruise is the best way to experience Hawaii! Every island has its own feel. Honolulu has been called "L.A. on a rock," complete with traffic jams and nightlife. Maui is quiet and Kauai is the lush paradise you've seen in every Hawaiian movie you can recall. In a week-long cruise, you can hike, bike, see live volcanoes and clamber through extinct lava tubes, water ski then snow ski that same afternoon, snorkel in the gorgeous Pacific, chow down on loco moco and shave ice, and a million other delights await. Or, you can simply sprawl on one of the rated Top Ten in the World beaches.

One thing you cannot do in Hawaii is find a bargain-basement cruise price. If you can find a cruise under $125 per person per day, I say book it. Decent deals can be had in the less-traveled window between Thanksgiving and Christmas vacation, when many Americans are at their busiest. The most cruise ships visit the islands in September and October, as cruise lines add in Hawaii as part of their repositioning plan after the Alaska season.

Many cruise lines begin their voyages somewhere on the mainland, and have several sea days before reaching Hawaii, where they visit a couple of ports, the passengers fly home. In my opinion, Norwegian Cruise Line has by far the best itinerary. It's the only cruise line to offer a round trip out of Honolulu, and never leaves the islands, including two overnight ports.

Because the ship is American-flagged, most of the crew and staff members are American citizens. I've heard people grouse that the crew was "not subservient enough" but really, slave labor is past. We've found the crew to be outgoing, friendly, efficient, and I liked not having to consider any potential language barriers that can occur on other ships.

NCL is also the only cruise line to sail year round, which might fit your schedule better. This itinerary is port-intensive, with no sea days at all; not a typical cruise, but if you want to *see* Hawaii, this is the very best way to go. No, NCL didn't pay me to recommend them. They should.

Hawaii's high season covers mid-December until May, when snow-bound folks' dreams turn to a tropical vacation. Prices are steepest around Christmas/New Year's, into January. Who wouldn't opt for a Hawaiian holiday? That's also when air prices are at their most expensive, sadly.

The rainiest weather hits the islands between December and March. I attended university in Hawaii, and quickly learned the Hawaii rain is not like anywhere-else rain. For one thing, it's violent, and sudden. You can be walking along in bright sunshine and fifty feet later, you're drenched. Storms pass as quickly as they began. I quickly learned wrap skirts are not the way to go. After a sudden rain, the water evaporates so fast, it often steams in a surprising updraft, not conducive to modesty. Whoops– up over your head.

August is when the Pacific storms kick up, if they're going to. While hurricanes rarely affect Hawaii, their fringes can make the weather uncomfortably hot and humid. But, hey, it's *Hawaii*!

Mediterranean

If you want to cover the most turf in Europe in a short amount of time, a cruise is for you. Even with relatively inexpensive intra-Europe flights, you'd rack up a scary credit card balance, seeing only half of what a cruise ship offers. Mediterranean cruises glide from country to country, showcasing a new and exciting port just about every day. Not all ports are near the highlights, however. I suggest booking independent tours to get the most out of your time.

The busiest season is May to early September, when both European and American families scramble to fill in the summer sailing dates. This makes for a nice cultural mix of passengers onboard, with plenty of kid-friendly activities. The downside is bigger crowds at all the sites, higher prices, and steamy temperatures that can drain the sightseeing energy of even the most dogged tourist. August can be a frustrating time to cruise, as much of Europe's population goes on holiday, leaving restaurants, stores and many popular sites closed. Yes, they go all at the same time. Because they do, that's why.

Our first Mediterranean cruise was in mid-September, and it was so incredible, I wrote a book about it. *Mediterranean Cruise with the Cruise Addict's Wife*. America is a baby country; we just don't have 3000 year old ruins! Temperatures were still plenty warm, but about twenty degrees cooler than the month previous. In Turkey, where daytime high reached 98 that week, I appreciated that. If it's hot enough to bake cookies inside your car, it's too hot to hike across ancient ruins made of heat-reflecting carved marble. Just my opinion, mind you.

The off-season in the Med takes in early spring and late autumn sailings. Besides being slightly cooler, you're likely to find fewer crowds, and lower prices. Private tours are easier to book, too. You might even find some great ones on the pier. Tour guides flock to greet passengers who wander off the cruise ships mumbling, "I wonder what there is to do around here ..." A handful of ships remain in the region year-round, while most reposition, making for some dirt cheap trans-Atlantic cruises.

Mexican Riviera

Known for touristy ports and warm weather, these cruise itineraries are in high demand with families and spring breakers. The most choices are in the winter, when frozen Northerners need an escape from Old Man Winter. February and March are prime whale-watching months, with tours costing less than a good burger at home. Summer can be unbearably hot, hot, hot. Summer has less cruise options, since most cruise lines reposition their ships to Alaska then. As they should.

Low/Shoulder Season covers early January and May, and again in October and November

Opt for the off season, if you can. A more adult-oriented atmosphere fills the place, as college student bow their heads over their text books once again. Early January and May cruises can be an especially good value, plus there'll be smaller crowds and fewer kids once school is back in session. The downside to January is the weather, ranging from hot and killer-humid to downright chilly. If temps dip into the 40s and 50s, it cuts into sunbathing time. Mind you, I've seen dogged tourists vainly trying to get a tan in that weather, to prove they actually went on vacation. Hmm ... I wonder if spray tans were invented to cater to those who have more sense than to don a bikini in 35 degree weather.

South America

High season is November through March, which is pretty handy for us Northern Hemisphere types. Remember, seasons reverse at the equator, so winter here is summer there. As for drains draining in reverse, you'll have to check that out for yourself.

The two primary South American cruising routes are the steamy Amazon near the equator, and the exotic around-the-Horn or channel cruises between Buenos Aires and Valparaiso, Chile. Cruises ply the area during South America's summer, but you'll encounter seriously varied weather that can change in an hour, swinging from mid-70s to low 40s. Pack a swimsuit, a warm jacket, and a flexible attitude. Plus, factor in altitude in ports. Once you leave the ship, I mean; ships, by definition, sail only at sea level. I respected a Cruise Director for keeping a straight face when a passenger asked her what was the altitude of a ship at sea!

During busy season, cruise ships fill up fast with South Americans on vacation. You remember your high school Spanish? You can also expect sold-out ships over Christmas, New Year's Eve, Easter and Carnival Week. Watch for bargains between Thanksgiving and Christmas. Yes, I know; that requires advance planning. So does most of the rest of your life.

You can expect to dodge the crowds by traveling in the shoulder-season months of April and October. I prefer to travel when there is less competition for top tourist attractions; not a fan of standing in long lines. On the other hand, as my mother often says, "There's room for us, too."

In the Galapagos, cruising waters can get choppy in August and September – not appealing for those prone to seasickness – but temperatures are fairly consistent year round.

Tahiti/South Pacific

Most cruises visit the islands May through October, but the South Pacific's high season actually occurs during the winter months. Ideal, for people sick of winter's icy grip. During the winter, the weather tends to be more favorable, with less rain and a slimmer chance of tropical storms, although the strongest trade winds usually kick up at this time. Bring a hat. This region's dry season dovetails nicely with June weddings and school summer breaks, making this itinerary popular with honeymooners. European and American families on extended vacations make up a good portion of the rest of the cruisers.

November through April is this area's low season, with much lower prices. Being summer (remember, it's reversed this far south), you'll run into the wettest time of year, when rain, temperatures and humidity all soar up the charts. However, ocean temperatures are still perfect for swimming. If you're looking for a place for a stunning backdrop on your rub-it-in-their-faces Christmas card, you'll find it here.

Choosing a Cruise Line and Ship

Large or Small?

Choosing the right ship can make your vacation brag-worthy; a bad fit can be as miserable as those cute new shoes that pinch.

Large and mid-sized ships are perfect for those who love loads of activities. If you are happiest when making crafts, playing group games, watching cooking demonstrations, or laughing at the Hairiest Chest contest by the pool, you'll enjoy a large ship. Carrying 2000 up to 6000 passengers at once, these ships have it all. Big ships have nightly Las Vegas-style performances with energetic singers in a large show lounge, along with magicians, jugglers, and live music throughout the ship. If go-go-go is for you, come aboard!

However, don't rule out a large ship vacation if you prefer solitude, especially if your favorite traveling companions want to try a big ship. Every large ship I have seen has quiet places where you can get away. Outside decks (away from the pool), the library, window seats in less-trafficked areas, and the upper decks are all great places to find a bit of breathing space. So is the promenade. Catch your breath, then you can go back to the excitement by the pool or that fabulous magic show in the theatre.

Oddly, the new giants carry hundreds more passengers, but I guess someone forgot to add extra elevators to the blueprints. I'm fine with taking the stairs, but not up fourteen decks. Long waits for an elevator can bring out the worst in some people. That rather large woman comes to mind.

Not judging, mind you, just stating the obvious: she was pushing 400 pounds, and not very fast. The elevator, with me inside, was full, full, full when it stopped on her floor. Etiquette demanded she wait for another elevator. Perhaps she had reached her limit. She announced, "Room for one more!" crossed her arms, and made a running leap toward the open door, like a linebacker. I said the elevator was full, and I meant it; she bounced off the front passengers like a rubber ball hitting a concrete wall. Perhaps the applause in the elevator was not polite.

Mid-sized ships have a lot going on, but not as much as their big sisters. Some try to mimic the glitzy offerings; I once narrowly missed being kicked in the head by a feathered dancer in a small lounge. Clearly, her act needed a bigger stage than the dance floor, the only venue onboard. Mid-sized ships have just a little less of everything than the mega-ships. Where a behemoth may boast thirteen restaurants, a mid-size ship may only have four.

I prefer mid-sized ships over the biggies. I like seeing familiar faces after the first couple of days, trivia games of forty rather than six hundred, crew members who have time to smile. Less walking is required onboard, every venue is less crowded, and it's easier to find my way around the ship, including now-where-was-that-cheesecake-place-I-found-yesterday?

Small ships may feature more off-the-beaten-path itineraries, going where large ships simply don't fit. With only a few hundred passengers on any sailing. the feeling is intimate, and interaction with staff and crew is more personal. Chefs may go shopping in a port, taking along a few passengers, and purchase local delicacies for the evening's dinner. Small ships tend to have more of a Be Where You Are feeling, as opposed to one-size-fits-all. Menus and entertainment showcase local foods and guest performers.

While nightlife may be non-existent, daytime activities can include watersports right off the ship's aft fan, personalized hikes to environmentally sensitive places unable to accommodate larger crowds, even glassblowing onboard. Most small ship cruises cost significantly more than the mainstream large cruises, but usually include shore excursions, all beverages, and free internet connection, at least when they're near civilization.

Which Cruise Line Is Best For You?

Most of the mainstream cruise lines are more alike than different. Cruise ships come in a variety of sizes and personalities. Mega ships, intimate-sized ships, adventure-oriented ships, decadent luxury ships, bare-bones ships with wilderness itineraries, river boats, ships that cater to families or singles or older passengers or outdoors enthusiasts or beach bums, some relatively quiet, some with non-stop activities ... it's all up to you! Just like the variety of humans on earth, you're going to be drawn to some more than others. It's essential you know your style of travel before you book.

If you seek culture and history, don't book the party ships. If you love to dress up, the barefoot-style cruises are not for you. If you're a foodie, some ships will leave you cold ... and possibly, hungry. Sure, you love kids, but do you want to be on a ship with hundreds of little ones, while you've left your own with Grandma, in search of romance? On the other hand, traveling with your three young ones who are the only passengers under age thirty is a problem waiting to happen. If you're a party animal, you're going to be bored silly on ships that offer a quieter, more sophisticated ambience.

While mainstream cruise lines are similar, each has its own quirks, strengths and weaknesses that could well be a deal-breaker for you. For example, Celebrity appeals to spa lovers and gourmet travelers, Carnival focusses on mass-appeal food and entertainment, Royal Caribbean targets active multi-generational families. Norwegian seems to be doing the splits, catering to both bargain hunters and celebrities, often on the same ships, with its ship-within-a-ship concept.

Let's look at some cruise lines' strengths, bearing in mind that individual ships and itineraries have their own vibe.

Frugal Cruising

If you're budget minded, you're not alone. It's up to you: go all out on a once-in-a-lifetime voyage, or economize and cruise more often. If you can do without a penthouse suite, and can be flexible with dates, deals of $40-$60 per person, per day, are not hard to find on many itineraries.

Carnival is king of the budget cruises, offering short itineraries and frequent promotions. If you live near a homeport, thus skipping airfare, you can easily book a vacation at sea without selling your firstborn.

Norwegian: Some of the lowest cruise fares I've ever seen have been on seven-day shoulder-season Norwegian cruises. You'd do well to get on their mailing list to find surprising prices and bonuses like free beverage packages, free internet, and free specialty dining vouchers on all but their very newest ships. Consider short sailings and repositioning cruises for the best value.

MSC Cruises: MSC Cruises is new to the North American market, positioning *Divina* in Miami and tweaking its European product for US cruisers. Hoping to lure new-to-MSC cruisers aboard, promotions and low fare offers abound. It's okay to be a little open minded. "Unfamiliar" isn't the same as "bad," as I frequently remind my grandchildren.

After More Luxury?

Nothing wrong with a splurge now and then
Regent Seven Seas Cruises might be the most all-inclusive line out there. While its fares are considerably higher than other cruises, they include pre-cruise hotel stays, nearly all shore excursions, gratuities, onboard alcohol and soft drinks, fine dining in main and specialty restaurants, extra attentive service, even branded umbrellas on rainy port days. No, really; I've seen them!

Seabourn is known for almost-mind-reading care of guests by its uber-attentive staff, who pride themselves on swiftly learning your preferences. Do you take lemon in your coffee, disdain cherry tomatoes, only drink soda at breakfast? Make your wishes known just once. If you don't want to think about a thing, this might be the cruise line for you.

Norwegian's Haven: NCL justly boasts of the Haven, a "ship within a ship" for high-class or high-spending cruisers. Ships with a Haven feature an exclusive communal area for the elite top suite guests with a small private pool, sun deck, fitness center, restaurant and/or lounge. The Haven suites all include butler and concierge service. Haven guests are free to enjoy Norwegian's big-ship amenities: multiple dining venues, a variety of bars and smaller venues offering top-notch entertainment. If you're a celebrity, or on the lam, you can have a wonderful cruise experience without ever leaving the Haven space.

Solo Cruises Have It Made

Going it alone? Be sure to read the section on solo cruisers

Norwegian: Norwegian is storming the market with its Studio cabins on its newest ships, proving that solo travelers aren't always overlooked. On Norwegian *Epic,* 128 solo cabins face a shared social space with large-screen TVs, snacks, a bartender, and a social organizer to facilitate meeting other travelers. Norwegian's *Getaway* has 59 studio cabins. *Pride of America* features just four studios, with a tiny communal living area. Bear in mind, for the price, you might be happier with a regular cabin, and requesting access to the lounge. Studios are *small.*

Crystal: Crystal entices solo cruisers with a wide range of onboard activities, including nightly singles get-togethers, dance hosts and low solo supplements. The onboard atmosphere is communal, with the line going out of its way to bring solo passengers together for meals.

Traveling With Children

Just about all cruise ships cater to children to some degree. These shine.

Disney: You already know Disney leads the pack for kids' entertainment, and at sea is no exception. Its ships offer nurseries for babies as young as three months, Disney-themed play areas with enthusiastic Disney-smiled leaders for preschoolers and school-age kids, and the obligatory Disney character interaction, including meet and greets, and Disney pirate parties for the whole family. Is it possible to overdose on Disneyness?

Norwegian's Freestyle caters to kids, who might not be up to sitting for two hours in the main dining room, or wearing scratchy dress-up clothes to meals. Buffets feature kid-height, kid-friendly sections, and the children's menu is wonderful. On the other hand, my two year old granddaughter disdained the kid menu, requesting extra plates of calamari for dinner. Nothing wrong with expanding one's horizons, and a cruise ship is the ideal place to try that.

Royal Caribbean: Royal Caribbean is one of the better family cruise lines. With entertainment that crosses multi-generational groups, look for innovative children's programming and expansive youth facilities. New partnerships with Mattel's Barbie and Dreamworks bring the characters little ones love onboard with parties, parades and photo ops.

Carnival: A kids' program for age two and up, sky-high waterslides and onboard aqua parks, plenty of free, kid-appealing food options ... What's not to love? Add in some of the largest family cabins in the industry, and lots of North American homeports. If your little ones are your top priority, this may be the line for you.

Taking the Teens

Not much worse than having a bored teen in your cabin;
much like a mosquito, the urge to smack 'em is real. A better
choice; Book a teen-friendly cruise.

Royal Caribbean: RCCL's tricked-out mega-ships
are a hit with older kids and teens, offering everything from
rock-climbing walls and onboard surfing to DJ classes, zip
lines, high-energy shows and late-night pizza. Teen clubs
bring kids together for parties featuring the latest in video
games plus disco and lounge space, presided over by teen-
friendly staff who know how to encourage wall-flower kids to
dive right in.

Norwegian: Norwegian's "Freestyle" approach is
ideal for teens, who'd rather not eat with strangers, or dress
for dinner, or be on time for ... anything. Entertainment is
abundant, with something for everyone. There's even teen-
only karaoke.

Carnival: Most Carnival ships have outdoor movie
screens, water parks with waterslides and soaker areas, ropes
courses and mini-golf, as well as dedicated teen and 'tween
areas where they can (safely) party it up. This cruise line even
offers active shore excursions just for 12- to 17-year-olds,
chaperoned by the youth staff.

Seniors at Sea

*Some of my favorite fellow passengers have 80-104 years in
their rearview mirrors! Just because you've had a lot of
birthdays doesn't mean you're too old for cruising.*

Holland America: Mature travelers who hearken back
to The Good Old Days of Cruising will enjoy HAL's cruise
traditions (afternoon tea, ballroom dancing), as well as
enrichment cooking and technology classes. Its wide range of
itineraries– one day to 108-day world voyages – offer plenty
of options for retirees looking for multi-generational trips or
long vacations to new places.

Cunard: Big on classic cruising, Cunard offers regular
transatlantic crossings on its flagship Queen Mary 2. Wish
you could relive the days of the great ocean liners? Come
aboard! Dress for black-tie dinners and formal ballroom dance
parties, politely applaud well-regarded plays or jazz concerts,
savor scones with clotted cream at afternoon high tea, and for
goodness sake, don't ask, "What is clotted cream, exactly?"
You just don't want to know.

Learning and Enrichment
*All of the mainstream cruise lines offer some onboard classes
or lectures, but these stand out:*

Oceania: Make a memory, and a delicious meal, at
the Bon Appetit Culinary Center's two-person cooking
stations. In ports, Culinary Discovery Tours take food lovers

on field trips to artisan cheese makers, local chocolatiers, vineyards or fish markets. Arts and crafts classes are offered by the artist-in-residence onboard.

Crystal: Crystal made onboard education a priority decades before the other lines caught on. Its Creative Learning Institute offers a variety of classes, including computer skills, golf and art workshops, as well as cooking demos, talks on political science and current affairs. They feature astronomy classes, held on the darkened upper deck, far from the lights of any city. Guest lecturers are onboard to talk about the local experience, making the next ports come alive before you reach them.

Cunard: Cunard provides top-notch enrichment programs, including a speaker series, and literary discussions. Add in acting workshops, gaze skyward with onboard members of the Royal Astronomical Society, and you may not want to get off the ship.

Ahoy, Foodies

Would you rather dine, or eat? Some cruisers rave about the elegant dining options, while others are happiest with a burger by the pool. If you're in the latter category, like The Cruise Addict, any ship will do. For true food fans, like me, read on:

Royal Caribbean offers its exclusive Chef's Table, a not-to-be-missed seven-course tasting menu with paired wines, and a signed, complimentary cookbook. Guests rave about it, insisting the experience is well worth the $75 fee.

Celebrity: Celebrity is all over the specialty dining scene with a variety of onboard restaurants, and the main dining rooms are almost as good. Sample Continental street foods on up to Italian delicacies prepared tableside, followed by design-your-own crepes.

Oceania: With world-famous chef Jacques Pepin's dishes in every onboard restaurant, you know your taste buds will be dancing. Besides superb cuisine in its main venues, Oceania offers Asian, Italian, and a steakhouse onboard, fee free.

Fitness Lover's Cruises

Afraid of getting out of shape on a cruise? All cruise ships have somewhere to jog or do sun salutations, but these add more ...much more!

Royal Caribbean: A boxing ring, ice skating, surf simulator, mini golf, sky diving, rock climbing walls, onboard zip lines ... What are you waiting for? RCCL organizes daily competitions on the sports court. Take advantage of the huge gyms with cardio machines, free weights and weight machines, or the classes on Pilates, cycling and aerobics. Need some quiet time? Hit the non-skid jogging track. Just do it quietly; I'm relaxing here!

Norwegian: First to add onboard bowling and water slides to some of its ships, NCL quickly stepped out with a rock climbing and rappelling wall. Newer ships feature ropes courses, dance classes, kick boxing, line dance classes and daily Zumba. Where else can you take high-kicking exercise classes taught by Rockettes-trained instructors? Large gyms, sports courts, and large-screen Wii tournaments in the atriums are sure to keep you on the go. On the drawing board: a two-story go cart track! I'm tired, just thinking about it all.

Interested In Water Sports?

If the whole point of an ocean cruise is getting up close and personal with the ocean, here's to you:

Luxury cruise lines such as Seabourn, Windstar, and Paul Gauguin feature water sports equipment free for passengers' use, including kayaks, jet skis, pedal boats, water skis, windsurfing boards, a variety of inflatables, and snorkeling gear. Some ships have retractable platforms right off the back of the cruise ship to launch water craft.

Several cruise lines offer a scuba program with both recreational dives and certification classes; you can actually certify during a cruise! Of course, swimming and snorkeling can be a real workout, and walking in sand is great for the leg muscles.

All The World's A Stage

Shakespeare had it right. Cruise ships' entertainment ranges from a solo violinist in an intimate piano bar to Broadway-type production shows, and you've already bought tickets!

Norwegian: NCL is near the top when it comes to innovative entertainment at sea. Partnering with land-based brands, passengers can enjoy both Blue Man Group and Chicago's Second City improv troupe. On some cruises, Second City even offers workshops, so you can hone your improv skills, or learn to tie a snake in a knot. That's a skill you didn't know you needed. All ships have jazz and blues clubs, celebrity musician impersonators, talented singers, production shows, and dueling pianists and comedians. Magicians, too; I'm still wondering how she moved that piano onto the balcony railing with no one noticing.

Disney: No surprise here: Disney knows how to entertain. Its onboard stage shows rival land-based theatres, showcasing a mix of original productions, laced with the catchy tunes, creative props and costumes, and favorite characters you'd expect from Disney. And don't forget the ship-wide Pirate Party, combining an interactive musical show with dancing, games, and fireworks shot right off the ship. Don't worry; they're biodegradable.

Royal Caribbean: RCCL pushes onboard entertainment options out of bounds! The only cruise line with Ice-Capade-style ice skating shows and water-based acrobatic shows also brings Broadway to the high seas with condensed versions of "Chicago," "Hairspray" and "Saturday Night Fever." Add in costumed parades down the Promenade and aerialists performing in the atriums of its Vision-class ships, and you'd better have your camera at hand!

Bring On the Night Life

After long lazy days spent sunning and exploring, who's up for a party?

Carnival: Carnival loves its Fun Ship reputation, and you can bet it glitters after dark. You're never far from a bar or dance club, and the casino is often the hottest place onboard, followed closely by the wild karaoke nights—which only get raunchier as the night goes on. Late-night comedy is a staple event in the line's Punchliner Comedy Clubs. Did you know George Lopez helps choose performers for Carnival?

Celebrity: If high-end drinking in a quieter atmosphere is more your style, you'll enjoy listening to live jazz while sipping craft beers at Michael's Club or settling in for a wine tasting. Something wilder? Try the Martini Bar, where juggling bartenders pour colorful concoctions. With live music around the ship, there's always dancing available in the disco or nightly parties.

Norwegian: From the bordello-meets-bowling-lanes themed Bliss Ultra Lounge to the ice bar on Epic (complete with parkas!), NCL offers plenty of specialty venues, and the staff keeps things hopping. Pack white clothes for the signature White Hot Party, the happeningest dance party aboard any ship. Nightly karaoke is a big thing on NCL, and it's memorable ... for one reason or the other.

Theme Cruises

You might love being part of a theme cruise, detest it, or not notice it's going on at all. The key is, be informed ahead of time! Think of a hobby you enjoy, a band you'd love to meet or an exciting activity you've always wanted to try, and there's likely a theme cruise for it.

Music is a big draw, including country, jazz, rock 'n roll, opera, and charters by bands, like a week-long concert venue. Favorite celebrity chefs, photography, crafts, financial whizzes, along with clothing-optional, LGBTQ, and other lifestyle themes, faith-based cruises, sports stars, family-only, and ships featuring well–known speakers, all make for popular cruises. With such a wide-ranging variety, theme cruises are a great option.

If your cruise features a theme, make sure it's one your whole party will love, because it sets the tone for the entire cruise. While Husband would revel in country music playing in every venue, I'd find it torturous, akin to non-stop fingernails on chalkboards. Amplified.

Some cruises have themes on a smaller scale, so many passengers might not even know they're there. I've encountered company retreats and business conventions in full swing, demos by famous chefs, break-out talks by famous coaches and authors. These groups might meet a few times per cruise, or every morning for three hours, and the rest of the time, they're on their own. Or they might be involved all day, every day.

I peeked in a conference room on a cruise some years ago. Taken aback, I stopped to peer in in more detail. Rows of long tables held sewing machine, while others were festooned with colorful fabric. Pieced quilt tops hung in various stages of completion from clothesline around the room. Head bowed over tasks, sewers were oblivious to me watching ... or to the rest of the cruise.

I ran into one of the quilters later on. She admitted they never left that windowless room except for meals, but exclaimed, "We get to take home a competed quilt at the end of the cruise!" I, too, enjoy quilting, but I do just fine on land. I'm not trading a whole cruise for the opportunity to sew.

Theme Cruises Can Be Broken Down Into Three Categories:

Full-Ship Theme Cruise: Make sure you really care about the theme, because it'll permeate every aspect of the sailing. Every onboard venue will be tied up with the theme, and every passenger can participate in the themed activities and entertainment. On a music cruise, this will stretch from the pool deck for concerts to the dining room, where special menus might be featured.

We disembarked a ship in Barcelona, with mere hours to spare. Back Street Boys were taking over the ship! Conference rooms packed full of bling and tee shirts, amplifiers as tall as the ceiling, crates of concert programs, giant decals on all the tables and the pool deck, banners and posters everywhere ...whew, that was close!

Our cabin steward admitted she was worried, after their morning meeting. "We're told to expect 95% ladies, almost all between the ages of 18 and 24, sleeping until three o'clock in the afternoon. My supervisor issued ear plugs to help us sleep. My cabin is on Deck *Two*– yet she assured me the music will keep me awake without them!" On that sold-out cruise, I'm sure those screaming young women made lifetime-sized memories. I'm glad I wasn't aboard with them!

Full-ship theme cruises can be either fully chartered by an independent company or offered by the cruise line itself. For example, Sixthman, a travel company focusing on theme cruises, offers fully chartered musical festivals, such as The Rock Boat and Cayamo. Throughout each cruise, passengers can enjoy concerts, themed activities and competitions and opportunities to mingle with performers up close and personal.

Cruise line partnerships include Celebrity's "Top Chef" Cruise, Food Network's cruises and Regent Seven Seas' annual Chocolate Cruise. These tend to appeal to a broader audience. If you are that audience, look them up. If not, do your homework to be sure you're not sucked into something you'd hate.

Partial-Ship Theme Cruise: Not all theme cruises engulf the entire ship. Special interest groups can book a number of cabins in different categories, and then market them to people interested in the activity. Trade magazines are ideal for reaching customers who might not otherwise cruise. Themes can range from scrapbooking to baseball to hearing a motivational speaker. These small groups usually don't impact the other passengers, although some of the public spaces may be taken over, at least part of the time.

Others allow cruisers plenty of downtime to indulge in their passions. For example, a golf cruise allows duffers to brush up on their skills with a cruise itinerary dotted with world-renowned courses, hardly meeting up at all, while a dancing cruise can be include all day/ every day classes in multiple venues for both seasoned fox trotters and beginners.

In the Caribbean, and again in Hawaii, we encountered bicycle marathoners on our cruise. A group of 30-45 of them had their fancy bikes stored in the cargo hold of the ship. In every port, the crew unloaded their bicycles, and off they went. While we lazily sprawled on Top Ten beaches and explored shops and quirky museums, they rode around the islands, 26 miles every single port day. It looked like great fun! We cheered them on as they rode off in the mornings, and the ship welcomed them back later in the day. Each day, they looked a little more tanned, a little more tired, and their numbers shrank as the cruise progressed. But the sense of accomplishment was tangible!

Theme-Inspired Cruise: Cruise lines commonly advertise themed sailings, but these tend to be regular sailings with some extra special-interest activities or guest speakers added to the usual programming. On these sailings, you might have a regionally inspired wine tasting, a well-known chef, or guest musical performers onboard. Paul Gauguin Cruises, for instance, features appearances by oceanographer and environmentalist Jean-Michel Cousteau throughout the year. On select sailings, Cousteau offers lectures and accompanies dives from the ship. Many cruise lines welcome special guests onboard its ships, ranging from well-known photographers to local brewers. Don't expect to find great bargains those weeks; they have their followings, you know!

Choosing a Cabin

Okay, you've narrowed down the cruise line and where it sails, and which cruise dates work best for your vacation. Good for you!

After itinerary, choosing your stateroom is one of the biggest decisions you'll face. You might not care all that much; some people simply reserve the cheapest cabin available at the time of booking, preferring to save their money for shopping or shore excursions. After all, once you're on the ship, you'll have access to the same food, main dining room, shows, activities, etc, that any other passengers attend. Sure, the fancy suites get some extra perks, such as reserved seats at the shows and perhaps an exclusive restaurant or VIP breakfast venue, but that's not for you ... right?

Stop a minute. I'm all in favor of saving money, but you can get a good price and still not have to settle for the lowliest cabin on any ship. Just hold your horses.

Other cruisers disdain the "lesser" inside and ocean view cabins, seeing them as "beneath them". Only suites and penthouses fall under their consideration. If ocean breezes in your pajamas is important to you, by all means, upgrade. If you're the type who keeps the curtains drawn every day at home, you'll be fine booking an inside cabin. If you really need a grand piano and more square feet than an average ranch house, you'll have to book one of the best suites onboard.

In Hawaii, we booked an inside cabin, figuring we'd be on shore most of the time anyway. We upgraded to a balcony for a last-minute great price. Exactly a year previously, my brother's family booked the biggest suite on the ship, and paid six times more; same cruise, same ship, same itinerary. I guarantee we had more fun than they did. I hear I'm fun to travel with. And frankly, I'm not exactly sure what to do with a butler anyway.

Either way is fine, of course. It's your vacation. Personally, I base my choice on the itinerary; for a lengthy trip, I want natural light. In warmer climates, I spend long hours on the balcony, reading, writing, watching the ocean. In frigid temperatures, I opt for an oceanview, avoiding the inevitable draft and wind-sounds from a balcony. For a short cruise, say, under a week, an inside is fine. For us, the sticker shock of a mega-suite isn't worth it. We like to go and do and see things, not spending much time indoors. If you're planning to lounge around and watch DVDs all cruise, you need to factor that in.

My behavior changes, I've noticed, depending on the cabin we book. If we have a smaller cabin, I tend to be out and about the ship more, participating, meeting new people, seeing the scenery from a 360 degree vantage point. You'd think cruises known for scenery, such as Alaska or the Panama Canal, would pretty much require a balcony. Nope. If you're holed up in your own little space, you'll miss the grandeur of it all. You're better off on the open upper decks, where you can experience the Big Picture. Regardless of which cabin category you choose, you'll still want to be on the top deck as you sail under the Golden Gate Bridge, past Kilauea Volcano, or out of Venice after midnight.

Almost as important as the size of cabin is the location on the ship. I'll cover noise in a bit. Overlooking this detail can be the difference between a relaxing vacation and more stress than you had at home. I know this all seems obsessive to a first-time cruiser, but you'll thank me later.

In addition to knowing your cabin options, you need to know yourself. Do you tend to get seasick? Do you prefer to nest peaceably on your balcony rather than hanging with the crowd around the pool area? Is being near that great piano bar important? Conversely, is your idea of a stateroom simply a place to flop into bed at 1:30 am? Are there certain amenities you're willing to splurge on, or can you simply not justify paying for unnecessary perks?

Some cruise travelers prefer their cabins to be near, or far away from, specific areas of the ship. Sun-worshippers might prefer an upper-deck location close to the pools and sun decks. Party people might want easy access to midships entertainment hubs. Travelers with mobility concerns may prefer a stateroom close to a bank of elevators. Those long hallways seem to grow longer as the cruise progresses.

You'll want to examine deck plans with great care. Adjoining cabins have a smaller loveseat or chair, rather than a sofa, to allow room for the door to swing open between cabins. The connecting door tends to funnel noise between the cabins, cutting down the illusion of privacy. They're fine for a family who wants to keep an ear on the kids; not so good for anyone else.

We lucked out in the Mediterranean, and received VIP status, to boot, by checking cabins carefully. Cabin #8500 on NCL's Spirit costs the same as any oceanview, but it's at least

40% larger, even larger than our friends' suite. There are only two like it on that ship, a funny configuration where the straight side of the ship tapers into the bow; not big enough space for two cabins, but much bigger than its neighbors. I'm a writer, and loved being able to spread out assorted papers and brochures on the wide open floor. The double closet was big enough for a hammock. No, I didn't pack one.

Before you book, look carefully at the configuration of the cabins you're leaning toward. Easy-peasy; these days, folks post pictures online of all sorts of random things, including last week's breakfast. Do a search for the ship's name and cabin number, and I bet you'll find yours. Seeing the cabin's bed configuration may be a deal breaker or a selling point for you.

I skipped this step on a cruise with my teen-aged daughter, plus I politely gave her first choice of bed on the ship. An older ship, the cabins were oddly shaped, with the beds at right angles. She wisely chose the one that let the ship's motion rock her to sleep, side to side. In rough seas, I lay awake all night, noticing my vertebrae expanding and contracting, over and over, as the ship's motion rocked me end to end. Felt like a weird internal massage. Not bad; just ... weird.

There are also websites that show the deck plan for every cruise ship; I'll list some at the end of this book.

Some staterooms are laid out sideways, giving more floor space. Some that sleep extra passengers have Pullman-style pull down beds from either wall or ceiling, while others have fold-out sofas. Both have advantages and disadvantages, same as anything else. Fold out beds disappear during the day, and your steward makes them up in the evenings.

We had this arrangement in Hawaii. We liked having a larger sofa during the day, but Husband had to climb over our sleeping daughter to get to the balcony first thing in the morning. No surprise; Daughter was grouchy. Folding the bottom third of the bed up the next day – with her still in it – didn't cheer her up, either.

On one cruise, my brother's daughter had a trundle-type bed that pulled up from under her parents' bed, effectively making the cabin wall-to-wall mattresses at night. They had to crawl into the bed from the foot, since there was no room to walk around the sides at all. Not ideal.

Pullman-style beds fold up into the wall or ceiling during the day, out of the way, but they're prime targets for bumping one's head in the night. You may not feel safe with the three-year-old twins sleeping in Pullman beds with just a short railing; some cruise lines forbid children under six from the upper berths, but may not tell you until after you board.

On some older ships, the cheapest cabins feature only one twin-size bed, plus an upper berth that pulls out of the wall. Leaving aside the obvious barrier to any planned romantic activity, I am not happy at the idea of wearing sequins to dinner and the show, then going "home" to what is essentially a bunk bed. If the words "cabin" and "bunk bed" are in the same sentence, the vacation's theme had better be "camping," not "cruising."

Location and Noise

Noise is a big factor in choosing a cabin; perhaps the biggest, if you hope to sleep at all. Back to those deck plans you go. Be aware of what's above and around the cabins at hand. RCCL's ships' centrums are like a wind tunnel for sounds. Their own website warns they funnel noise, music, and serious vibrations from every live performer down the hallways, rattling the first 6-9 cabins on every floor in from the center of the ship. Every night! We could feel the walls shaking from the beat as we walked by. I doubt those people slept much in there. You might think a wild party is fun, and it is, if you're part of it. Not so much if you have an early tour in the port the next day. Mind the fine print before you book!

If your ship offers family suites, keep in mind that families are likely nearby. Read: there's the potential for screaming children, or loud parents singing "The Farmer in the Dell" at all hours. If you'd rather avoid the ambient sounds of a large family group, then perhaps it's best to relocate away from that area entirely. Of course, you could end up sharing a wall with loud adults, and you won't know that until you board.

You might think you're home free booking a cabin above or beneath the theater. They often cost much less than similar cabins in their category, and after all, the shows are all at night, right? You plan to be out and about every evening, at the nightclub, piano bar, or the shows themselves.

Stop! Yes, shows are in the evening, but rehearsals can be all day long, causing your cabin to reverberate to the beat. Even if you really love the Hermit's Hermits, you're not going to relish the review band practicing "I'm Into Something Good" for hours on end.

It's the pool deck that often causes the most noise problems. If you don't want to hear scraping chairs at the crack of dawn or yee-hawing pool parties until the wee hours, go down a level. Other problematic cabins are those situated low and at the back (because of their proximity to engine noise, vibration, and the anchor) or low and forward (because of the bow thrusters).Some passengers shy away from elevator banks, but we find those areas generally quiet.

If you can, identify where crew-only service entrances are located. Those tend to be the blank spots on the deck plans. You may not be thrilled to wake every morning pre-dawn to the sound of cabin stewards loading their cleaning carts for the day's rounds, or moving heavy sound equipment for the next show.

The metal stairs which room service runners, cabin stewards, and various other staff use at all hours of the day to get around throughout the ship can get very noisy, too. Even worse is the galley: bumping, rolling carts, shouting and stomping around the clock. Those lovely croissants you enjoy for breakfast are made by bakers whose shift starts at 2:15 a.m., and they don't tiptoe as they work.

In your planning, don't forget the cruise ship has an engine room. While some people call that infernal humming "white noise," insisting it puts them to sleep, the constant buzz of machinery makes others batty. Passengers on the lowest deck are most likely to hear engine or even anchor sounds.

Oh, the anchor! It may not show up on deck plans, but plot out where the anchor is located in relation to a bow cabin you're thinking about booking. Anchors are dropped in nearly every port, often before passengers are up and about for the day. That loud grinding noise'll startle you out of your skin if you happen to book a cabin behind that wall. Husband likes to nap midday, and in the Caribbean, it presented a problem. The crew took advantage of the long port days to practice lifeboat drills, all week. The grating sound of the davits put him into peel-me-off-the-ceiling mode every time.

Take into account the anchor hole, even when you're not in port. In seas higher than about six feet, the waves hitting that hole can make it sound like you're inside a cathedral's bell tower, and the thing's being rung about every fifteen seconds.

Of course a storm can arise any time, any place, but if you're going somewhere known for rough seas around the time of your cruise, consider this: ocean view cabins in the lower decks can be very noisy as the ocean's waves collide with the ships' wake. It's dramatic to watch from an upper deck. From an outside cabin on a lower deck ...think about how a washing machine sounds, with your ear pressed against it.

It's widely agreed that the best passenger deck to choose is one sandwiched between other passenger decks. You might run into noisy neighbors, but it's unlikely they'll have access to pots, pans, or an industrial sound system.

Cabin Types

All staterooms come with basic amenities, such as the services of a cabin steward to clean your room and turn down the beds, soap and shampoo in the bathroom, individual climate control, a safe, a chair, a closet. After that, upgrades and added perks are nearly limitless.

A typical cabin, regardless of category, is referred to as a "standard" unless there is something about it that makes it different, such as a loft, or special locations (aft or forward), handicapped accessible or a designated family cabin.

On most cruise ships, there are essentially only four types of cabins. The rest are just variations thereof:

Inside cabins have beds, drawers, closet(s), a private bathroom, a tv, a safe, and usually a desk, a chair or sofa or two. They often include a refrigerator and a small extra table. There's no window or natural light, but clever lay out, mirrors and colors make them seem larger than they are. Inside cabins on the lowest decks are usually the least expensive on any ship. Although passengers prone to seasickness swear by the lower deck cabins, they're also the farthest from the common areas such as the pool and lounges. Insides can be found on almost every deck, across the hall from staterooms with windows or balconies.

Oceanview cabins and standard inside cabins are almost identical in size and layout, except oceanviews have a way to look outside. The view can be clear or obstructed, either partially or nearly entirely, and the price reflects that.

You might want to check out the size of the window. Ocean views on lower decks only have portholes, while upper decks cabins typically have large picture windows.

Balcony cabins have a small private outdoor space (balcony, obviously) that you can walk out onto, except for French balconies, which open, but have nowhere to stand. They're like a floor-to-ceiling window, with a railing. The main benefit here is fresh air. They can be the same size and layout, or smaller, as the inside and oceanview staterooms. Be sure to read; does the cabin's listed square footage include the outdoor space?

Suites are cabins with "more." That "more" could be as simple as a balcony, or a little more square footage. Some suites come with added amenities, perhaps a bathtub, extra table or chairs, a dividing curtain, even another bedroom or bathroom or two. Why two cabin mates need three bathrooms baffles me. Even more puzzling was the bidet in a suite I saw. I don't get those. My behind doesn't need a drinking fountain, thankyouverymuch.

All other types of cabins, including solo and mega-size suites, fall into these categories. I want you to book the cruise that suits you best. Let's look at advantages and disadvantages a little closer.

Inside cabins have a bad rap, but they're the first to sell out on most cruises, after suites. The ship may sail with vacant penthouse suites, but insides, almost never. The main complaint is the size. In reality–always a good place to start–

insides and ocean views and many balcony cabins are often the same size! They just lack a window. Clever mirrors and color schemes make the space feel more open.

We took design concepts like that into account when we were designing our house, too: the cathedral ceiling, bow window, and kitchen pass through make our house feel more spacious. We toured a mobile home sales lot, because tiny home designers know how to maximize space, if anyone does.

Apparently, the cruise designers had the same thought. Cruise lines do all they can to make inside cabins feel bigger, including some that even boast electronic "balconies" or "portholes." Those are just big screens with a constantly playing scene, but they sound impressive, don't they?

You have to consider your cruising style. Some travelers only use a cabin for sleeping and showering. If you enjoy being out and about, involved in ship's activities, and meeting new people, an inside cabin will suit you fine. On the flip side, if you're the type who only wants to hole up and watch movies on tv, you might be uncomfortable in an inside cabin. You do know you can do that at home, right?

The obvious advantages to an inside stateroom is the price. Passengers swear they sleep best in the total darkness afforded by this category. Insides tend to be the least expensive cabins on any ship, and can be located on any deck. While they're great if you like to sleep in– no morning sun to disturb your sleep– that can be disorienting. Your alarm clock reads three o'clock, but is it the midday three o'clock or the middle of the night three o'clock?

A trick is to turn the tv to the Bridge Cam channel. It shows what's ahead of the ship, whether that be a morning sun or pitch black night. It also plainly shows the weather, saving you putting on your swimsuit to head to the pool if a rainstorm blew in. There's nothing wrong with darting up to an open deck to take in your surroundings first thing in the morning, but please get dressed first. No one wants to see your Winnie the Pooh pajamas.

We've booked inside cabins, and enjoyed those cruises at least as much as other ones with fancier staterooms. Remember, once you step into the corridor, you'll see the same shows, attend the same games, classes and actives, and dine in the same dining room as anybody else. You may well opt to save money here, and spend it on things that matter more to you, such as a tour, spa or casino.

Don't spend it on bingo; you can do that at home. Did I tell you about my friend Nat? She cruised Alaska twice: once with her mother, the second time with me and Husband. When she was with us, she kept raving about how beautiful Alaska was, how nice the ship was, how much she enjoyed the towns. Finally I asked, "Nat, didn't you say you'd been here before?" Sheepishly, she admitted she and her mom had spent every day playing every bingo game on the ship, long hours every day! Yes, she "won" $34 at the end of the cruise, but you can't measure how much she lost.

Oceanview cabins can also be referred to as Outside staterooms. Outsides are often nearly identical to inside cabins, in size and lay out; the only difference is that an inside category usually has a mirror or painting where the window is in an oceanview cabin. "Obstructed" category oceanview cabins often cost about the same as an inside stateroom. The main difference is the window or porthole. Portholes and windows do not open; you can see out, and get natural light, but no fresh air.

"Obstructed" cabins have a window, but may be totally or partially blocked by something, usually a lifeboat or part of the ship's structure. Often, you can't see anything if you look straight out, but if you're willing to climb onto the sill, press your face against the glass, lean *way* left, and look down, you might be able to see a slice of the sea, if the wind is blowing just right. Or, you might book a cabin that is in the shadow of a lifeboat that doesn't block the view at all.

Obviously, an unobstructed view is just that; wide open to the outside world. They tend to cost more than obstructed or insides. Either can be a good choice if claustrophobia is an issue, allowing you to look out anytime.

I tend to book oceanview staterooms on most of our cruises, just for the cost savings. More savings = more cruises. I enjoy looking outside first thing in the morning. One memorable day as the ship pulled into St. Thomas in the Caribbean. Awk!—we were surrounded by warships! American ones! My first thought was "Oh, no, who are we invading *now?*" Second thought was calmer: 'Oh, wait, those are *our* ships, and America has a navy base in the US Virgin Islands." Whew–clearly, I needed to wake up fully before looking out the window.

Balcony cabins are the next step up the cost scale. They may be the same size or even smaller than an inside cabin, but they have a sliding door that opens to the wide world. Ocean air anytime you want it– this is the biggest reason to get a balcony stateroom. Even if you can still *see* the ocean through a window in your stateroom, or *imagine* it with an interior stateroom, there is nothing like feeling the sea breeze as you cruise from port to port, especially in warm places.

Balcony cabins can be located on almost any deck, in any location (forward, midships and aft), though some cruise ships will not offer any balconies on lower decks. We've booked balconies on Deck Nine, and still the sea mist made sitting out there a soggy, salty experience. Balconies range in size from small affairs barely able to squeeze in two chairs and a tiny table to huge wraparound decks with outdoor dining tables and private hot tubs.

And take into account how private *private* is; often, balconies are layered, allowing people above you to look right down onto your space. Others are open to the wrap-around deck of the ship, letting people walk within two feet of your balcony table, all day long.

What's my opinion of balcony cabins? Depends where the ship sails, and the climate. In warm weather, stepping outside first thing in the morning to greet the new day can't be beat. In chilly places, I've found myself cramming paper wads in the door frame to stop the drafts.

There are a few times when I consider a balcony pretty much required. One is if you or a traveling companion come down with Norovirus symptoms. Being incredibly contagious, you can plan on being confined to cabin for a few days, even if you're not the sickie. To face being cooped up inside an inside cabin for days on end makes me want to scream. It's even worse if you need to air out the room, and can't. The obvious issue here is that Noro is unpredictable; you can't plan on getting it months in advance. If you could, wouldn't you forego the cruise?

If you have a baby who needs an afternoon nap, having a balcony allows you to settle the little one, then step outside to read or talk in Big People voices without disturbing that much needed sleep.

Ah, the bliss of letting the sounds of wind and sea lull you to sleep! You might want to prop open that balcony door as you sail, but cruise lines aren't so thrilled about the idea. Warm air coming in will cause your cabin's air-conditioning to work harder, wasting energy, or shut itself off. Plus, open the door to the corridor while the balcony's door is open, and you create a wind tunnel in the cabin, which will send all your dining reservation notices, cruise ship dailies and art auction advertisements flying everywhere.

A bleary-eyed crew member told me the fire crew had been up several times in the previous night. Leaving the balcony door open can set off the smoke alarm when the sea and air temperatures match up just right. Poor passengers-! It'd be disconcerting in the middle of the night, to have the ship's fire crew barge in.

A "**hump**" **balcony** is one located on some ships' mid- ship bulge. They stick out a bit, giving unobstructed views of aft & forward. Hump cabins are the same size or smaller, but the balcony space can be a little larger. Be aware that, due to their central location, noise from the ships' heart can be a serious issue. And while you can see farther, other passengers can also see you ...not ideal for mid-day nudity, should your thoughts aim that direction.

Aft staterooms are always in demand. Those are the balcony suites that overlook the rear of the ship. You can only see where you've been, not where you're going, or even where you are currently. I don't use rearview mirrors in cars much, either. Why should I? I've already been there! Well, there was that one time Husband chased me fully eight city blocks before I noticed him. Aft cabins offer stunning panoramic 180 degree views of the ship's wake. Some feature wraparound balconies, on the rear corners of the ship.

Aft balconies may be covered, or may not, and can become unbearably hot on clear sunny days; more so, since they are protected from the wind. These tend to be quiet, since they're located at the very end of the ship, there's no reason for passengers to pass your door on the way to their own cabins.

Forward balconies are always attached to expensive suites, and many people won't sail any other way. While the suites themselves can be about the same size or smaller than anywhere else on the ship, the front-facing balcony is *big*. In some cases, it's as big as the stateroom itself. And if you prefer to see where you're going versus where you've been, a forward facing balcony might be the right fit for you.

As with the rest of your life, there are a few disadvantages. The sprawling forward balcony is directly under the watchful eye of the bridge 24 hours a day, and it's totally open to the elements, including rain and beating-down sunshine. When the ship is underway, it's much too windy to leave the balcony door open. Indeed, they have warning signs about the heavy door slamming. Forward staterooms can feel closed-in, since there's no window and the door to the balcony is heavy metal, not glass as on other balconies.

The balcony can be can be unusable (even locked) for lengths of time during bad weather. Forward-facing balconies are also, well, at the front of the ship, so you will feel more motion as the ship cruises through the water. They can be noisy, due to the ship's hull cutting through waves, but you might love that. If you long to see what lies ahead, this cabin category might be great for you!

Cove balconies, also called hull balconies, are closer to the front of the ship. They're not available on all ships, but keep an eye out for them. Cove balconies cost about the same or less than an oceanview, generally, but include a private outdoor balcony. Besides being closer to the sea, they also can be larger than regular balconies. The quirk is, size and shape can vary wildly.

These balconies actually part of the hull of the ship itself, much like a load-bearing wall in a house. Often they have extra steel around the sides (part of the ship's structure), like a window frame with no glass, or a solid metal wall a foot or more off the floor. Regular balconies have clear, plexiglas from the floor to the railing. In a cove, you may need to stand up or lean over to get a full view of the sea.

We've booked ones that just had a sturdier-than-usual roof, otherwise a wide open verandah. Instead of those flimsy sound-amplifying dividers, cove balconies have solid walls on each side. Another advantage is that you can be outdoors without the wind blasting you. They're also a little safer for families with smaller children, and the privacy can't be beat.

French balconies are found on everything from mega cruise ships to smaller river cruise ships. As expected, they're also found on apartments all over France: I noticed last year. They're not actually balconies at all; more like floor-to-ceiling sliding glass doors that open to a railing. If there is a deck at all, it'll be very narrow, but most times there is just a handrail and no platform to step out onto. On ships that have French balconies, you'll find reasonable prices. It's nice to be able to open the doors to let in fresh air, but forget about sunbathing, unless you have a six-inch waistline.

Another type of balcony cabin, pioneered by RCCL, is the inward-facing **Boardwalk/Promenade** types. Instead of seeing the ocean out one's small balcony, they overlook the Boardwalk center of the ship. That's a busy hub, lined with shops and restaurants and pubs, featuring live music, dancing, even parades, right below. It's a great location for people watching, but note: they can watch you right back. Sheer curtains must remain closed all the time, and it's too noisy to keep the balcony door open. They do let in fresh air, and if you book one at the aft end of the ship, you can catch a glimpse of ocean by leaning out a little bit. If you're a parade lover, or want to see the water show from above, here's your chance, for not much more money than an oceanview cabin.

Virtual balconies are not balconies at all, but I'd better mention them anyway. It's an 80-inch high-definition screen in interior staterooms that spans nearly floor to ceiling on some newer ships. Ship-mounted cameras play real-time images of the sea; Disney even has characters randomly swimming by. The "balcony" includes a virtual railing, too, and natural sounds associated with the views are piped in. You can control the volume, which you can't do with the real ocean. Cruise lines that offer this odd option insist customers love being able to watch sunrises and sunsets while at sea. Tired of it? Curtains can be drawn to conceal the HD screen.

My opinion? Thanks for asking. A "virtual balcony" is a giant tv screen, not reality. The advantage is the price is not much higher than an ocean view cabin ...   only without the actual ocean view. We are living in seriously weird times, people.

Other Cabin Categories

Besides insides, oceanviews and standard balcony staterooms, which can be remarkably close in size and shape, there are a few other categories of cabins onboard. Solo-only Studios and suites top the list.

Norwegian pioneered **Studio** cabins, and some other cruise lines are jumping onboard, so to speak. All studio cabins are inside–no natural light–and all are, shall we say, intimate. As in, a tidy space-capsule size. If you're at all claustrophobic, you won't like it. Some say the studios are coffin like, and worse when the lights are out. If you are a large person, you won't fit comfortably in the mini shower or in the separate toilet area. One good thing; you can't hurt yourself when you stub a toe, because it's too small to get a running start in a studio cabin.

Studio cabin's sinks are too small to wash out your dainties; it's smaller than your basic loaf of bread, and not that deep. Storage is extremely limited; studios have no drawer space at all, and just a couple of narrow shelves in the bathroom. And the bathroom ... regular standard-sized North Americans may not be able to completely close the shower door. Yes, it's that small.

The desk area is tiny, but with no chair provided, it's probably not suitable for anything more than heaping stuff that doesn't fit elsewhere. Want to use your laptop? You'll have to balance it on your lap, while sitting on the bed. The closet is merely an open rod, with room for very few hangers, and not even a door. That might work on a two-day cruise, but on anything longer, where would you put your clothes?

The advantages include a private studio-only lounge with a big screen tv, and room to sprawl out, with 24-hour-a-day snacks, a bar, a daily happy hour, and staff on call ready to give suggestions and facilitate meeting other single passengers.

The cruise line's idea is to attract more single passengers who formerly balked at paying the extreme supplemental fee for a solo passenger in a double cabin, often 200%. However, do your due diligence in price comparing: on many sailings, the cost of a studio cabin on NCL is still higher than paying double for a regular cabin, and it's a third the size. For many people, the additional space, larger bathroom, desk, having your own tv, etc, is well worth booking an inside cabin over a studio.

As for the exclusive lounge, many solo passengers in other cabin categories have asked for a key card to the studio lounges, and it's been granted. That would allow a solo passenger to enjoy the benefits of meeting other solos, while having a space big enough to spread out in at the end of a day.

Look into the solo cabins if you desire, but bear in mind that for the space and price, you might be happier in a regular cabin. Or find a buddy to share. Surely, you could scrounge up a friend.

Suites come in all shapes and sizes; all feature balconies. They range from NCL's over-the-top 5,000+ square-foot, three-bedroom Garden Villa suites on its Jewel-class ships. Other suites may come with dining areas, wet bars, deluxe bathrooms, walk-in closets, multiple levels and even pianos.

On the other end, a mini-suite (found on nearly all ships) is often just a bigger version of a standard balcony cabin, sometimes with a small sitting area with a loveseat or convertible sofa. The mini-suites also usually have a curtain that can be drawn to separate the sleeping and sitting areas. Read carefully! Some suites include fancy perks such as exclusive VIP dining, a butler, and a set-apart seating at shows, while others are suites in name only.

Living Onboard

A cruise ship cabin is a compact space, likely smaller than most hotels you've stayed in. Although, the quaint hotel room we booked in Venice comes to mind. The whole room was about fifteen inches larger than the bed, so tight we literally had nowhere to put our suitcases. We set them in the bathroom. When one of us wanted to walk around the bed, the other had to step into the hall. The hotel owner sheepishly acknowledged it was smaller than American hotels, "But since you're going on a cruise, you should be grateful because, certainly, your cruise ship cabin would be much smaller." Turns out he was wrong, by at least half. Still, we were there for the charm, and it certainly paid off! The light fixtures in the room were genuine Murano glass, the windows were leaded stained glass, and that made up for the fact that the windows didn't close. My morning shower was a quick one, as the warm water was interspersed with the cold rain and wind from a sudden storm!

The first thing to do is explore your stateroom. You'll want to unpack, and planning where to put your Stuff is first. You do what works best for your cabin mates. In our case, I get all the shelves and cubbies on the right-hand side of any mirror, and the right-hand side of the closet, while he gets the left-hand spaces. The middle is for shared items, like the first aid kit, the binoculars, and the cameras. There's a bit of height disparity between us, a full sixteen inches. Thus, Husband takes the tall shelves in the closet, where I can't comfortably reach, and I take the lower ones, where he can't comfortably bend. We've been married a long time. It works.

There will likely be little shelves and cubbies in unexpected places. Look behind mirrors, under the bed, in drawers. I've even found storage space inside a footstool. Utilize the shelf under the bathroom sink. You might consider bringing a collapsible square bin for larger items, such as hair appliances. Counter space can be quite limited, but there's plenty of storage tucked behind the mirrors, including the ones in the cabin itself. Look around! And don't forget to check everywhere when you pack up to go home.

Up to five crew members can pass through your cabin during an average day: cabin steward, bar person, maintenance, etc, and any one of them might prop your door wide open while they duck around a corner to get something they need. Anyone walking by can see into your cabin, and a less than honest person also sees an opportunity. Be sure to keep your valuables tucked away, out of sight during the day, preferably in the safe, if they fit. If they don't fit in there, at least tuck them under something, perhaps your shirts in the second drawer down. It's always best to charge your electronic gadgets overnight, when you're guaranteed no staff or crew will come in.

I select a place on the wall, and turn it into a command center. I'm careful to choose an out of the way space, so Husband's broad shoulders don't brush it as he walks by. Not that I'm calling the Cruise Addict big, mind you, but when he needed a MRI on his shoulder a while back, he went to see the Seattle Seahawks' team doctor, who sent him elsewhere for the test. Apparently, the guy has shoulders broader than a pro football player.

Walls in ship's cabins are made of ferrous metal, assembled at the boatyard like Lego blocks. They hold magnets! I pack strong magnets to display the itinerary, plus tickets, notes, and invitations right at a glance. I need to know where to meet our private tour guide in port, and what time was the Captain's cocktail party anyway? On complicated cruises, I've seen people make full color spreadsheets to keep track of every hour, stuck on the wall. Plainly, "relax" is not on their schedule.

Bring a few magnetic hooks if you'd like. They create more hanging space for scarves, wraps, and assorted sunhats.

Why not just use tape? Cruise chip crews detest the stuff. It leaves behind sticky residue that takes more time than they have to clean off between cruises. In dire cases, it can also remove the finish from wooden or metal cabin surfaces.

Another item they dislike is those over the door pocketed shoe holders. In rough seas, or when people pass them in normal comings and goings, the darn things can slide, marring the door over which they hang. Disney forbids their use; some other cruise lines charge $100 if they spot one in your cabin.

Personally, I just don't like them. I tried to like them, really I did. I carefully arranged cards, combs, maps, brochures, sunblock, folded hats, flip flops, clothespins, and other dinky items in the pockets, then hung it over the bathroom door. The next person who walked past knocked it off the door, scattering the contents far and wide. Filled it again; same thing happened. On the third time, I carefully wadded the offending hanger up, and stuffed into the cabin's waste basket. I have my limits.

The next day, our cabin steward "helpfully" retrieved it, smoothed out the wrinkles, and rehung it. He must have tiptoed out, because it didn't fling itself off the door until I walked in. Back in the trash. The next day, the steward repeated it, and the stupid thing flew off the door again! That time, I emptied it, folded it neatly, and stuffed it into my tote bag, where it waited until the next port. I threw it in a trash bin miles from the ship, nevermore to be seen. By me, at least!

I've had some vast closets on some cruise ships, but that's not always the case. Slide an open suitcase under the bed to provide extra storage space for bulky items you don't use daily, forming a big drawer. You may only need your thermal jacket that one day when you get up in the middle of the night to greet the sunrise at Haleakala, then not again until you reach Glacier Bay.

Clunky snorkel gear also comes to mind. I don't want to rent it, because I don't know who all has had their germy mouths on it. Stuck in a corner of the cabin, that gear can grab a person by the ankle in the night, and fling them across the cabin without warning, causing them to knock down their laptop on the flight past the desk and land with their nightshirt over their head. Theoretically, of course. Best to tuck the gear under the bed, where it's contained.

In many modern ships, the door key is designed to turn off electricity to your cabin when you're not in it, thus saving power to lights you may have left on. True, you don't need to keep the lights on in a vacant cabin. You might want to leave your electronics charger actually charging, and probably the air conditioning on, as well. Smart travelers know the way to circumvent this is to simply slide another card into the slot; a library card, business card, even folded paper will do; whatever it takes to break the turn-off circuit.

In our travels, the standard rule is: Nobody Poops In The Cabin Bathroom, Ever. The public restrooms have far better ventilation. If you choose to violate this rule, you'd better pack some sort of air freshener. A cotton ball soaked in vanilla or lemon extract is nice; pack it in an empty prescription bottle for transport. If you opt for a spray scent, pick something neutral, like Fresh Linen or Clean Cotton. You're going to be mighty tired of Ripe Banana or Garlic Bread scent before the cruise is over.

Have you heard of Poo-Pourri? Again, I should get paid for product placement. It's a spray used before pooping that "leaves a lovely lingering scent" as opposed to a smelly bathroom odor. It might be worth the purchase price.

Along those same lines, yes, the bathroom tissue on a ship isn't the four-ply super soft stuff you're used to at home. It's a sight better than the hospital variety, which has visible woodchips, if you hold it up to the light. No matter how tempted you and your tushie are, *don't bring your own toilet paper*! Ships systems run on a vacuum system, and it's touchy as all get out.

Think of going to the drive-up window at the bank, and those vacuum tubes used to send money and checks back and forth to the teller. It's basically the same system on a cruise ship, only without the money. Only the quick-dissolve toilet paper made especially for use with the system will do.

There can be up to eighty bathrooms on the same line. Flushing the wrong TP, as well as tissues, apples, hamsters, and so forth, can block up all eighty toilets. Bringing your own roll might seem like a good idea, until you get the bill for repairing the toilet system you broke.

The vacuum systems work well, until they don't, but even on a new ship, they can make odd noises. I'm pretty sure at least a couple of the bathrooms on our cruises were haunted. It sure sounded like that; heavy breathing and moans from inside the bathroom walls!

Before I leave this topic, here's a quick fix for unwanted toilet odors, as if there was any other kind. Pour a coffee pot of water down the shower drain, all at once, to create a barrier in the ship's vacuum system. No coffee pot? Find a similar size container. Don't overthink this.

Traveling Companions

You can travel in a huge group or alone, or like most people, in groups somewhere in between. Regardless of your traveling companions, remember there are hundreds of other passengers onboard, and every one of them is there to enjoy the cruise. You automatically have something major in common! Be friendly, greet people, strike up a conversation in the elevator, offer a hand, ask an opinion. Not sure which specialty restaurant to try? Need another couple for your trivia team? Wondering what the animal bobbing in the ocean is, and do flying fish really fly? Simply asking, "Is this your first cruise?" or "Have you been to (the next port) before?" opens up conversations–and you already love the topic!

A cruise ship can feel like a community — one where well-traveled cruisers help out those who have little idea what to expect. On every sailing I've seen, person after person has been helpful and friendly. Veteran cruisers will know more than a first-timer, and most are very willing to share tips and hints. Sure you'll encounter the random snob, but they're so rare, you don't need to worry about it.

Just my opinion, mind you, but I think it's very helpful to go on your first cruise with someone who's cruised before. Of course, by reading this book and my first, *Cruise Tips from the Cruise Addict's Wife,* you'll know more than just about any other passenger. Even so, there are so many little tips and hints that a first-time cruiser could miss. Plus, it's fun for the experienced cruiser to see the trip through fresh eyes.

I like cruising with others, but I admit it's much easier with just Husband. We can coordinate with just a sticky note on the mirror: "Meet you at two o'clock by the dolphin statue". Sometimes traveling with a couple dozen people can feel like sheep-herding all week long.

On the other hand, our trip to Europe included twelve of us, and we had such a remarkable time, I wrote a book about it. *Mediterranean Cruise with the Cruise Addict's Wife.* Being with folks who can tell time and were as enthusiastic as we are made it great fun. These friends were the best traveling companions.

There are advantages in traveling alone: You have no one to wait for or catch up to, you can snore, stay up all night, read in the buff, come and go as you please, and you're totally free to meet new people and strike up friendships. On the other hand, you have no advocate to speak for you in case of medical crisis, there's no one to tell that funny thing-that-just-happened to, no one to compare notes with, no one to share experiences with. Still, you also have no one insisting you go to that lecture with them, turn off the light, change the tv channel, order something besides ice cream for dinner. It's a trade off.

I had lunch with a nice man who was on leg four of a 104-day cruise, a series of back to backs. He loved traveling solo, and listed a number of new friends he made. He insisted, "I already know all about my friends at home. Same old stories! Meeting fresh faces and hearing fresh stories for the first time is magic. I like the freedom to do what I want, when I want and how I want."

Solos, as well as crowds, can participate in ship games and activities. Single cruisers can often join a private tour through cruise line's roll call on CruiseCritic.com, or book through private tour agencies themselves. Many tours will happily add other passengers to fill the van. Splitting the cost makes sense. That's a great way to safely explore a port; safety in numbers, as your mother always said.

In a group or family, you have witnesses, someone to say "Hey, where's ole Whatshername?" if you don't show up, people who understand you and your background, maybe even care about your likes and dislikes and opinions. It's admittedly harder to walk away from obnoxious passengers if they share your last name or, worse, your cabin. In a too-tight group, you could feel tied down, having to be accountable for your whereabouts. You're less likely to do something foolish like jump into the Quest game, or the marriage game onboard, or join a conga line, knowing you'll have witnesses in the audience.

If the group is large, rather than booking one big dining table, consider a couple of smaller ones. Six people at a table can converse much easier than twelve, and you can switch seats the next day if you desire.

We did this when traveling with a family group of fourteen, spanning three generations. The teens and older kids staked out a table, and the adults ate at an adjacent one, with in-laws and outlaws carefully arranged to avoid friction. The waiters were less frazzled, too.

In a group, you're less likely to speak to other passengers, or met new people. If you're traveling with another couple or two, you already come equipped with your own trivia team or team for any other game. Pros and Cons, same as anything else.

A couple of friends of mine decided they were not going to buy Christmas gifts for their extended family one year. Instead, they gave them all a seven-day Mexican Rivera cruise and airfare; all 62 of them. The whole group was excited (and not one returned that gift, let me tell you). Even using the help of a trusted travel agent, the process was a bit overwhelming. They opted not to plan anything together; once they were on the ship, they were on their own.

The biggest non-commercial group I've heard of was a friend's daughter's quinceanera celebration. As I understand, it's a giant party to welcome the girl into young adulthood, without having done anything stupid in her life, like running away or getting a big pink mermaid tattoo on her nose. This party had 128 family members and friends on a seven-day Caribbean cruise. Coordinating all those guests was so bad, the cruise line issued the girl's mother a walkie-talkie, same as the crew had. Everyone had a lovely cruise ...except Sophia's mother. She took a vacation the following week to recover, all by herself.

Nearly every cruise line will toss in one free cabin if you travel in a group of 15 or more. If you end up being the designated plan-maker, be sure to ask about this. If you're going to have the headache of coordinating everybody's schedules and preferences, you may as well have the perks, too.

Even with people you love, it's often best to make arrangements to meet one or twice a day, rather than being joined at the elbows, 24/7, if you wish to be on speaking terms by the end of the cruise. Say, everyone do their own thing, then meet for dinner, full of fresh stories. Other events during the day are by individual choice.

On an extended-family cruise years ago, my mother-in-law insisted everybody get together to play card games every afternoon, from lunchtime to time to dress for dinner.

I balked, firmly. "No, I will be busy at that time, but I'll meet you all for dinner." She didn't need to know that my version of "busy" included wave-watching, reading on the upper deck, and admiring fluffy clouds overhead. We don't spend all day every day together at home; it's not healthy at sea, either.

Regardless of group size, it's best to get your expectations out in the open ahead of time, because the great wide ocean is no place for a heated dispute. When we booked a Southern Caribbean cruise with friends who we liked but were not really close to, I had reservations. We agreed to meet up for dinner, but quickly discovered we had more in common that we thought, and loved being together.

We even had a compatible travel speed; in ports, we'd tour in the morning, have lunch, then my Husband and Melissa wanted to go back on the ship. Bryant and I had more left in us. We'd go back on shore, shopping, exploring, happily meeting local residents.

Bryant is a great haggler, and that's not where my talents lie. If I wanted to buy something, I'd hand him money and he'd talk the vendor down. I felt a little awkward the first time, but I did ask Husband's opinion first.

"Are you okay with me going into a foreign country with a cute blonde's husband and having him buy me things?"

In the Mediterranean, our group of twelve had a great time together on private tours, but we barely saw one another back on the ship. I think we had dinner together twice, onboard. No one felt attached at the hip; in Rome, eight of us were together, in Tuscany, only four, in Florence, half of the group went off by train to climb the Tower of Pisa while the rest met a tour guide. By respecting each other's independence, we had a great time. We're already planning our next big cruise together. Having said that, we've traveled with others with whom we didn't mesh, and I have zero desire to travel with them again. We just don't tell them when we're cruising.

If you have a kid, you might think about packing a cousin or a good friend along. Keeping track of one child or three takes about the same effort, and they'd probably love having a buddy along. It's like twins. One baby takes 24-hour-a-day care. How much more could two take? I'd recommend a medium-sized, well-behaved child you already know and love a lot. Our kids loved having near-their-age cousins on several cruises.

Traveling alone or with your favorite someone is also good. You're more likely to interact with new and interesting people if you don't move like a mob onboard. When else will you have the chance to join a trivia team with a Texan nuclear scientist, a teacher from New Zealand, a Canadian jockey, and a well-known novelist? Sit in your own group, and the chance will pass you by!

I happen to love Husband, and we travel well together. Even so, we have no problem going off on our own during a day. I'll attend a class he doesn't care about, or take a book up on deck; he'll nap or play a game without me. I don't enjoy jugglers or magicians. Husband does, so off he goes. Sometimes he reports "It was great! You would have loved it," but I don't believe him.

Bottom line: it's everybody's own vacation; we just happen to be on the same ship going to the same ports.

My friend found herself on a cruise ship with her new in-laws just days after a knock-down, drag-out family brawl in which the mother-in-law called her every name in the book, and made up three new ones. Being too frugal to cancel at the last minute, the four of them went on the cruise. In an attempt to keep the peace, the husband/son took a deck plan of the ship, and drew a thick, black marker line end to end. For the whole seven-day cruise, the old folks stayed on the port side of the ship and the younger couple on the starboard, only seeing one another for emotionally icy dinners.

As for sharing a cabin, keep in mind compatibility before you book. Is your friend a slob, a night owl, noisy? In my case, Husband is nocturnal, and I'm not. We've had to lay down some rules, such as "Feel free to wander the ship in the middle of the night, but you'd better not slam the door on your way out." In exchange, I try to be respectful when he finally sleeps, usually mid-afternoon.

We learned this raising our son, who first 'slept through the night' (four consecutive hours! yippee!) at age thirteen. Yes, *years*. For sanity's sake (ours), we made rules for him once he was old enough to climb out of his baby bed and wander the house all night. No touching exterior doorknobs, don't do anything that generates heat, and be very sure you want to face the wrath of exhausted parents before you wake horizontal people. At that, sanity was iffy those first years of his life. Mercifully, he grew up, has a family of his own, and still sleeps a lot less than most humans. No longer my problem.

Traveling With Kids

Cruises are one of the best options for multi-generational vacations. Children and teens love cruising! And it's easy to take them along. Sure, there's some extra prep needed, same as any other age, but it's certainly doable. We've cruised with family members aged 16 months through teens and beyond, up to elderly in-laws. I gotta say, kids are easier, and less demanding.

Little people are remarkably adaptable, so long as they have what they need: generally, a somewhat predictable schedule, food at regular intervals, enough sleep, and family people who love them. Throw in a set of clear expectations and their favorite teddy bear.

We all love a good surprise, but knowing what to expect can avoid needless angst. Hearing The Plan For The Day is critical at all ages, not for just young people. In our family, we keep a running commentary on what to look forward to, and the required behavior.

On a cruise, it might sound like this:

"We'll get on the ship as soon as it's ready. Before then, we'll wait in a line for a while, and you may play with the new hand puppet in my bag. If we have to wait too long, I'll give you a snack. There will be people all around us. They don't know us, so we'll need to use our quiet voices. As soon as we get on the big ship, we will go exploring. You're going to love the kids' play place."

or

"Okay, in five minutes, we're going to put on clean clothes and go eat dinner in the fancy restaurant. You may choose what you want to eat. I wonder if they'll have a nice salad for you? Use your best manners, stay in your seat, and remember not to disturb other people. You're a nice child, so act like it."

Our tiny granddaughter loved cruising– and she blossomed! She was a shy one year old, who surveyed the world from the safety of her daddy's shoulder or peeking out from behind Mommy. By Day Two, she confidently chirped "Hi!" at everyone we passed. Soon she learned that smiling and blowing kisses would earn her a grin. By the end of the week, she confidently chattered to everyone in sight. The crew doted on her. A lot of them have children of their own, and they go months between seeing their families.

When you cruise with children, your experience will be different than when you go with a group of rowdy friends or on your honeymoon. Younger children require a calmer pace. Push them too far, too fast, and they go off like– well, like an overtired three-year-old. Think of it like going to Copenhagen versus downtown Hong Kong. Not bad, just different, with less late night dancing, and more walking the decks. Go with the child's needs, and you'll all be happier. If you power through naptime and delay meals, the chances of a meltdown increase exponentially, and I don't mean just a wailing baby.

Getting our toddler granddaughter to sleep on a ship was a problem, because she was simply too interested in all that was going on around her. I think she was afraid of missing something. On Night Three, we figured out that a bedtime snack (pound cake and pickles from the buffet suited her; yes, she chose that every night) helped, then we simply bored her to sleep. We circled the decks with her in her stroller, carefully avoiding interesting parts of the ship. Long stateroom corridors with identical doors were dull enough for her little mind to stop racing.

Despite the minimal challenges of traveling children and teens, new places are always more interesting when seen through kids' eyes, more engaging when examined with their earnest curiosity, and certainly funnier when narrated by their wicked sense of humor.

Home life is hectic these days, with school, homework, sports, after school activities, invasive electronics and friends, not to mention the parents' own distractions. Some cruise lines now offer teen-only shore excursions, and we've met people who blithely left their children on the ship while they took off in port for the day. Not for me! If we're doing something fun, I want my family with me.

When we're on vacation, a lot of what we really want to do is be together. Time on a cruise ship, in a confined geographic area, can do wonders for your family life. Being together long enough to talk in full sentences, trying new foods together, sharing new experiences, breaking the daily routine, can do magical things for a family, and effects often carry over to home. Who knows, this might be just what you need to remind you you *like* one another!

We've found private tours to be invaluable for our family, giving us the flexibility to stop whenever we needed for food or a bathroom break; we control the itinerary. Being stuck on a bus is never ideal with a child who's Done, for either the child or the other sixty-two passengers.

Of course, in any port, you can book active shore excursions like kayaking, hiking, cycling, snorkeling and diving, or calmer ones your kids would enjoy. Glass blowing and a chocolatier might interest a teen. Asking a local, "Where's a playground?" will let a little one get some wiggles out. Giving older kids a say in what they'd like to see and do makes everyone happier. A family shouldn't be a dictatorship, within reason.

In our family, we emphasize history and people when we travel, so museums and local cultural centers call to us, along with hiking, and local food. It's essential that our family knows the world is bigger than our home, our town, our circle of friends who are similar to us. We wanted them to be interested in taking their place in the world, and not as spectators. It's paid off: our daughter-in-law frequently marvels at how much our son/her husband knows about the world. "Anywhere we go, he knows more than the tour guides!"

Onboard Activities for Kids And Teens

It's not easy for a kid to be miserable on a cruise ship! In a safe environment, children of all ages can have fun mingling with those of their own age. What a fantastic opportunity to meet others from around the country or around the world–just like their parents or grandparents. When else can your ten-year-old play games with a peer from New Zealand or Spain?

I had to laugh at my younger brother, years ago. The five-year-olds ran and played for hours together in Mexico. I asked, "How can you play so well together, when you and Miguel don't understand each other's language?"

Eyes wide, he gasped, "We *don't?*"

Ships feature expansive play areas with separate venues for young kids, 'tweens and teens, and often a nursery/play place for the youngest cruisers. All cruise lines have something to interest kids, while family-oriented ships have huge facilities that often include multiple play areas for the youngest cruisers, teen hangouts and discos, kiddie pools, waterslides, arcades and kids-only deck space.

They're strictly divided by age. Most cruise lines cite insurance reasons as the reason age groups are not allowed to overlap. This can be a challenge if you have cousins six months apart, in separate groups.

Eager to draw in multi-generational families, cruise lines constantly add new and exciting things for young people. Elaborate water parks, onboard zip lines, rock climbing, surfing, roller skating, learning to DJ and watching parades, sky diving, even a two-story go-cart track at sea; a child would have to put serious effort into being bored!

Happy kids= happy parents, which makes for happy repeat cruisers. With that in mind, cruise lines constantly improve their children/teen offerings. Kids clubs are included in the price of the cruise. Led by trained youth counselors, daily organized games, contests, karaoke, scavenger hunts, arts and crafts projects, sing-alongs, pajama/movie nights, dance parties or simply supervised play make it hard for many children to pull themselves away.

Some lines have partnered with outside sources to offer unique programs, such as acting and juggling classes, hands-on science experiments, and cooking lessons. Children can spend as much or as little time as they want in the kids' clubs, either participating in activities or just hanging out. A few times, I've passed by, wishing I could join in. Who wouldn't love to make their own pizza and a tour of the galley while it's baking, in your very own chef toque?

When you cruise with kids of any age, work with the cruise line. Often, you'll be greeted by kids' group staff as soon as you usher a child onto a ship. They watch for young ones, eager to let them know what's available onboard. There's often an introductory session for kids and parents to meet the kids' clubs staff and get acquainted with the facilities.

It's better to sign up on Day One, even if you're not sure your kids will want to go; there's no requirement to attend the program, but at least get on their radar. Buddies get acquainted on the first day, quick friendships form right off, so make sure your kid is there. By Day Two or Three, they'll be The New Kid. You know it's harder to fit in once groups have already formed. This is critical, especially with teens. Missing this important social opportunity dooms your kids to being outsiders and robs them of the chance to be cool; akin to losing a limb for adults.

More Tips for Cruising With Kids

Unless you have someone doing all your cooking and cleaning at home, a cruise will let you spend more quality time with your baby than just about anywhere else. You definitely need to plan well and pack carefully, but it's soooo worth it.

If you have kids who will be taking naps, you will really appreciate the extra space and killer view you get from a balcony room or suite. While being stuck in an inside cabin through naptime might make you nuts, reading on a balcony a few feet from your sleeping child is awfully relaxing.

Bring the child's favorite stuffed animal or a couple of favorite toys; it's best to consult them. Pack diapers and wipes, formula if the child is not breastfed, bottles (disposable bottle liners are handy). I suggest making a pit stop at a store on the way to the port, so you don't have to lug all the gear on the plane. Diapers, when available on ships, are expensive, and may not be your favorite brand.

Make sure whatever you need for your toddler, including children's medicines, like pain relievers and colored band aids. You can't count on the ship to have these, and if a new tooth erupts or a small knee gets skinned, you'll want to have it at hand. I draw on band aids; I'm no artist, but anyone can draw a happy face, tree, clouds, ladybug, etc. That, plus a kiss, heals owies faster.

You'll be surprised how many diapers can fit into the outside pockets of suitcases, and along the sides/between clothes inside. The nice thing is they can't get hurt, so it's easy to stuff them everywhere. Or take them out of the box and pack the plastic packages of diapers that are still packed together extremely tight. They do take up some room that way, but it'll free up space to put in souvenirs on the way home.

Many little people hate showers. Some parents recommend bringing a blow-up bathtub or baby pool for bathing, but other say it's too much hassle. Keep in mind the showerhead in the ship's bathroom is removable. Instead of expecting a child to enjoy being pelted by a heavy shower, take it off and gently rain on your baby.

Worried about your child falling out of bed? I didn't. They won't fall out; do they fall out of bed at home? Our eldest son had a crib, which he used as a trampoline. Our two youngest slept in twin beds from age one on. I found cribs took up too much space, considering we mostly used it as a really big stuffed animal corral. Each toddler fell out of bed once or twice, then developed fine spatial awareness. Ask for a portable baby crib when you book the cruise, if you need one.

For older kids, you'll most likely reserve a cabin with either fold-out sofa or a fold-down bed. All upper beds on cruise ships have a rail, but they vary considerably in length, from most of the bed to just the head area. A foam pool noodle under mattress serves as a nudge to a restless sleeper to not roll farther. A rolled bath towel serves the same purpose. You could also wrap a big towel around the bedrail, then tuck it under the mattress. If your child is pretty young, or particularly squirmy, make sure you book a cabin with fold out sofa instead of a Pullman-type bunk.

Some little ones balk at using a Big People toilet; likely a fear of falling in and slipping down that little hole at the bottom. If your kid uses a potty seat at home, you might look into buying a folding one for the cruise, or packing their regular seat. A cruise is a long time to going without Going. A folding travel version is also good for the car later on. You never know when a need will strike; usually right past the "Last Exit For 12 Miles" sign. My parents used to keep a covered metal coffee can (empty) in the trunk, but that's probably not practical on a cruise ship.

I've heard some parents complain because young children are not permitted in any of the pools onboard unless they're completely out of diapers. Makes sense to me—who wants to swim in a toilet bowl, even one with lovely scenery? They insist, "My kid will be miserable if they can't go in the water!" Our solution with the toddler was easy: if she doesn't know it's there, she won't beg to go in it. It's easy to detour around a pool, especially with an easily-distracted child who's under three feet tall. "Ooh, look at the pretty ocean!"

Laundry can be an issue. I'm always amazed at how one knee-high person can generate more dirty clothes then two adults, but you know it's true. You can wash out their doll-sized clothes in the sink, but for extra messy items, spring for the ship's laundry service. Bibs are the worst. Try the new disposable bibs, or just secure a linen napkin around your child with safety pins, then leave it on the table after a meal. Nobody objects; the ship's laundry runs 24 hours a day anyway. Those cute bibs from home will be nasty after a week in your laundry bag.

Take along some painter's tape to baby proof the cabin. It doesn't leave residue, making it perfect for taping up cords, and covering electrical sockets.

You need to keep a close eye on your small fry, especially once they're mobile. There are stairs, fountains, and all manner of dangerous things all over a cruise ship for a child to explore, and those big venues have few doors to keep the child confined in a given space.

Be courteous to others in the theatre, but don't think you have to miss all the shows with a child. A small one might even sleep through it, in Mommy's arms or in a stroller at the back of the theatre. Sit on an aisle in case you need to make a quick run for it.

One of my happiest memories was of our little granddaughter, who could barely walk, dancing up a storm during a musical performance. She was enthralled by the music, and her dress swayed like a bell over her chubby legs. I stayed in the back of the theatre with her in case she complained; that only gave her more room to dance. I'm telling you, there are few things more joyful than a happy little kid letting loose.

Parents can also use the Divide and Conquer method of entertainment, if the show won't interest a child. Aerialists, music, dancers, ice skaters, variety shows will likely appeal; a comedian may not. One of you go to the early show and one to the late show, while Baby-Doll gets tucked into bed at a decent hour.

I recommend a baby carrier of some sort. There's a lot of walking on a ship and in ports, and little legs get tired fast. A front or back baby pack and an umbrella stroller will make everyone happier.

Food and Drink

Food-wise, cruising with babies is easy. You can get all the milk you need, and there are tons of choices for your little to try at all meals. Cereal, yogurt, eggs, oatmeal at breakfast; cooled soups, steamed veggies, pastas, mashed potatoes, soft meats at dinner; you may not need those little jars of baby food. Toddlers can find something edible on any buffet or menu; yogurt, and hard cooked eggs are available anytime, whether or not they're on the menu. Older children can choose from either the children's menu or regular one. On the ship with our toddler, our waiter brought a fruit and cheese plate every night, as soon as we sat down. It's a nutritious way to stave off imminent starvation.

I'm not a fan of Typical Kid Food. Even a picky eater (I'm not a fan of those, either) can find some interesting, albeit plain, menu items. Roast chicken is much healthier than fried chicken nuggets. Baked fish, pasta, fruit, salads, baked potatoes, mashed potatoes, rice, and steamed vegetables are all common choices, readily available. Let them new things, too. Shrimp or eggplant may be their new favorite food, but you won't know that if you confine them to yet another grilled cheese sandwich with fries.

Our young daughter sampled tuna tartare, escargot, duck, venison, and every vegetable she saw. Our two-year-old grandchild surprised the waiter by politely requesting a double serving of calamari, telling him, "I like the crunchy tentacles best." The ten-month-old at a nearby table ate only black olives every evening, which her parents stuck on her fingertips. I hope she had had a proper meal before the main dining room.

Encouraging kids to try new things is part of travel! Let them rise to expectations; it may surprise all of you. We travel to be away from the routine of home, after all.

You could wait for room service, but if your child needs a snack Right Now, it's better to be prepared. Take a banana and a couple of those little boxes of cereal from the buffet at breakfast to tide a kid over until dinner.

Cruise ships stock little, if any, prepared baby food, so bring your own baby food pouches/containers, and favorite baby snacks if you child eats them. For older kids, bring snacks from home. Granola bars, nuts, raisins, juice boxes, crackers are great.

If your child's at That Age, pack sippy cups from home. Lidded cups aren't available anywhere on cruise ships. Dollar stores often sell multi-packs of cups. For that price, it's no loss if you misplace one. Did you know even very young babies can use a straw, if it's short? They're used to sucking on anything in their mouth, and that's how a straw works.

There's no reason to give a baby a straw, but you never know, that could come up in a ship board trivia game.

Nothing wrong with taking a couple of small kid books to the dining room, either picture books to entertain little ones, or a thin chapter book for beginning readers. It'll keep them happy, and they're much less annoying than electronics.

You're parents; you'll figure this out!

Electronics

One of the tasks that signals I'm Really On Vacation Now is the act of placing my cell phone in the stateroom's safe. Sometimes I hear the old Southern spiritual "Free At Last" in my mind as I sigh and set the lock. In our modern society, it seems many people are tethered to social media, cell phones, and other electronic gizmos. Did you know you can get clinically addicted to those little pixelated screen?

The only time I turn on my cell phone is in a port. Usually, this is fine. There was that one time, however ... While I walked down the gangway into San Francisco, my cell phone rang. Uh, oh; the principal at our little granddaughter's school said she had broken her collarbone, her parents were not answering their phones, and could I come pick her up right away? NO. I'm a thousand miles away! By the time we reached the cable car terminal, I'd made a few phone calls and an aunt was on her way to get the poor child to a doctor.

While I'm guilty of sighing at people posting their lunch on Instagram, I *get* the whole electronic thing. I'm a writer, so you can bet I travel with my e-reader, tablet, laptop, extra keyboard, cameras, and all the chargers they require. But sailing out of convenient cell tower range brings a sense of delightful freedom. Just think, for the duration of the cruise, I can speak to others and expect eye contact!

With all of the electronics we tote around with us these days, most people find cruise ship outlets to be sadly insufficient. One per cabin is the norm on all but the newest ships. You may want to ask your cabin steward. Sometimes there's an extra outlet hidden behind the TV or under the bed.

Onboard, and realize you forgot your charger? Chargers are the number one item left behind by hotel guests, and it's the same on a cruise ship. After you mentally kick yourself, track down your cabin steward. They just may have a universal charger you can borrow.

I think one of the nice things about cruises is that cell phones are "roaming" on cruise ships, making their usage crazy expensive. On ocean crossings, they may even be out of range of any cell tower. TV satellites, too. Not to worry; the bridge always has a satellite phone if needed.

I find it refreshing to be away from the constant cell phone noises. Being able to talk to people instead of one of us constantly checking the little screen is healthy. On Day Six of a trans-Atlantic cruise, I was startled to encounter a young man staring at his IPhone screen intently.

"Withdrawals?" I politely inquired.

"Nope," he grinned, "Camera."

Ah.

If you're high on the transplant list, or just can't be without the darn thing, check with your cell provider before you leave home to ask about the roaming charges for your destination. Your plan may already include calls and e-mails throughout the U.S., Caribbean, or even farther afield. I found calls to be costly in the Caribbean, but texts were free. Puerto Rico and the US Virgin Islands are part of America, although they sure don't feel like Minnesota. Your cell phone should work as well there as at home.

Can we do without the internet for a few days? Even with discounted packages, going online shipboard is not cheap. Your best bet is to unplug.

Many lines offer free minutes if you sign up for an Internet package on the first day of the cruise. Standard rates are 75 cents per minute, though packages can lower that to about 40 cents, and loyalty perks offer free or discounted limited use. On some ships, you buy blocks of time to use as you see fit, say 30 hours for $45, and you can log on and off at will until the time is used up. Royal Caribbean sells internet in 24 hour blocks, and must be consecutive. That's 8 a.m. to 8 a.m. the next day, straight through. I find this difficult and wasteful; who's going to be on the internet all night long?

Some ships offer packages, but be sure you read the fine print, same as everywhere else. To get the most out of your internet access dollars, stop by the ship's Internet cafe and ask the crew member working there one simple question: "What do I need to do on this ship to get the most out of the internet connection?" A frank answer will greatly maximize your online experience.

The newest ships tend to have the latest satellite system installed, which is nearly as fast as the rickety old dial-up internet connections. On most ships, the internet is not fast enough to watch movies, and you can't video chat with your cute grandkids at home, even from the middle of a 15-day trans-Atlantic crossing, even if you really really want to. It'll do for email.

A faster way to send an email, without choking on using up your minutes, is to compose an email, or three, on a word-processor program. Get online, cut and paste your epistles into your email program, press send, and they're sent in mere moments. If you're a slow typist, this can save you a lot of money.

On more port-intensive cruises, ask a crew member where they get free internet connections in port. Anxious to contact their families at home, they all know. You might check a public library, a coffee shop, or even ask a hotel clerk to send a quick email. Any visitor's center or information booth can also direct you. Many ports have Wi-Fi right in the terminal.

You can always bring your laptop or device ashore and look for a bar or café with a Wi-Fi sign in the window. You may be able to get the password for free for the cost of a coffee or beer. Or, in the case of Husband in France, a cheeseburger and pomme frites. We still tease him about the big blob of mayonnaise on those french fries.

Instead of emptying your SD card online every night, consider dumping them onto thumb drives, and then upload them at home or in your post-cruise hotel, the one with free internet service. Uploading photos onboard the ship, at that speed, will rack up internet costs fast.

Traveling With Special Needs

Just because you have a difficulty arise, doesn't mean your cruising days are behind you. With some extra foresight, the world is still open. Cruise lines do their best to accommodate passengers. Whatever your situation, you're not the first to deal with it; it's likely the ship already has a plan in place to make traveling more comfortable for you. Just about every cruise company has a department dedicated to special needs. Look on the cruise line's website, searching for "special needs" or "accessibility" to see what's available. There's a limited number of high chairs, portable cribs, extension cords and everything else, so make your needs known as soon as possible, with a reminder email about 35 days before the cruise.

Contact the cruise line directly for help with: allergies, CPAP, baby beds, infant life preservers, kosher, vegan, or halal meals, scooter, shower seat, elevated toilet seat, wheelchair accessible/ handicap cabin, as soon as you book. Other special needs include: distilled water, sharps container, service dogs, cribs, high chairs, extension cords for CPAP or other medical needs. In some cases, a passenger may be required to have a traveling companion. Those are not supplied by the cruise line.

Some needs are pretty much built in to every cruise. With very few exceptions, your cabin can be reached via elevator and you can dine in your choice of accessible restaurants each night. You also have plenty of entertainment options that can accommodate you, including theatre seats accessible without stairs, and wheelchair parking seats.

Gluten free and sugar free foods are available at every meal, along with vegetarian options, but kosher meals need to be ordered ahead of time. Note: they're not fresh, but frozen meals heated and served on disposable plates.

Even in common-sense cases, a problem may still rear its ugly head. On our last cruise, one of our tablemates was taking a break from chemotherapy, and needed high-nutrition shakes every morning. She had packed the ingredients, powders, and potions. Although she had doctor's order in hand, and had notified the cruise line well ahead of time, the cruise line confiscated her Magic Bullet blender, which was required to make the shakes. Yes, blenders are on the Forbidden Items list, but with fragile health, she needed it. This was a very serious matter, made worse by the fact that she could eat very little else.

She made calls, protesting politely, to no avail; Security and Guest Services would not budge. Finally, on Day Two, the Hotel Manager himself stepped in. Every morning at 7 a.m. thereafter, he'd personally bring the blender to her cabin, along with juice and fresh fruits, hoping to tempt her appetite. The cabin steward was under orders to remove the blender as she made up the room each morning, and return it to the Hotel Director's office.

The needlessly complicated kabuki dance went on for the rest of the 16-day cruise. Notifying the cruise line's Special Needs department in writing at least 35 days before a cruise, then following up by phone, is the best you can do. Once onboard, make as much of a fuss as required, but mind your manners. The squeaky wheel gets the grease, but it ends up ... greasy.

In the case of a severe allergy or major physical or mental issue, you may weigh your options and decide cruising is not for you. I get no kickback from any cruise line; if you opt for camping to keep your child away from potential peanut-allergy contamination days from a hospital, go for it. None of my business, mind you, but in the case of a known issue, I'd rather be within shouting distance of help.

Cruise ships offer a small number of accessible staterooms, so book early if you need one. Generally, a "wheelchair- accessible stateroom" has wider entry doors and a roll-in shower with a bench, while a "modified accessible stateroom" offers a shower-only bathroom with low thresholds. "Accessible" cabins include a lighted doorbell for hearing impaired passengers, along with lights that flash during emergencies, bathroom grab bars, lower closet rods and automatic doors.

Your gear has to fit, so don't hesitate to ask for a larger cabin if you need it. Equipment cannot be stored in hallways, stairways or public areas because of safety regulations.

The first day onboard includes a mandatory muster drill, and all elevators will be unavailable at that time. Some muster stations are cushy; most seem to involve a lot of standing, after making one's way up or down several flights of stairs. Notify the ship right away, and your cabin will be assigned to an easily accessible muster station, with seats. Hearing impaired or blind passengers can also be assisted, if their needs are made known. In case of emergency, the ship has crew assigned to evacuate passengers who have limited mobility. You want to be on that list.

Service dogs are usually permitted onboard but might not be allowed to disembark at all ports. Check with the cruise line to determine what documentation is needed so arrangements can be made to accommodate the animal's needs. Litter boxes are often placed in nearby crew stairwells, but don't even think about asking a crew member to walk your dog unless a hefty tip is involved!

The medical center onboard will have a few crutches and wheelchairs, but they're for onboard problems, like the woman who broke her leg on Day Three, playing volleyball. Don't count on one being available; better to rent one ahead of time.

Passengers can rent scooters and wheelchairs from companies such as Carevacations. com, specialneedsatsea.com, disabled-world.com, and others. You can arrange for each of these companies to deliver wheelchairs, scooters, oxygen converters, and other equipment right to the cruise ship. You don't even have to go through the cruise line; they're used to these items being delivered.

You may have needs you consider too minor to mention. Mention them anyway. If you need to take medication with a meal, at least six hours before bedtime, late seating dining is not for you. Rather than hoping the cruise line will change your dining time, simply speak up. You're not the first problem they've encountered, or the last. You're probably not even the most interesting.

We pack power bars. Although I wouldn't eat them in a normal day, in an emergency, they're a life saver! When *Anthem of the Seas* had its bump-in-the-road a while back, when food was not able to be prepared or served, passengers were given free range of the stateroom mini bar. That ran out quick. Next, candy bars and bananas were delivered to a few cabins, but not all.

In the case of a child, or elderly person, or a diabetic, if you're not on the Medically Fragile list before the crisis arises, things can turn bad, fast. Remind the ship of any needs as soon as possible once you're onboard. You'd be wise to make a beeline for Guest Services.

Be aware of limitations in ports, as well as onboard. About a third of the world's ports require the use of tenders, small boats that ferry passengers from the ship to shore if no pier is available. Climbing down stairs, stepping onto a rocking boat, and back onto the dock requires some agility for anybody, and may prove impossible for some passengers. Tenders are typically not wheelchair accessible. Be sure to talk to the cruise line ahead of time, so explore other options, such as a different itinerary. It's no fun to miss out on a port day.

Ports themselves can be a challenge for mobility-limited passengers. I found Europe to be quite difficult, and I'm as mobile as anyone else. Tall, uneven staircases were everywhere! I don't think I found a single restroom that was on ground level, except the hole-in-the-floor one in Istanbul. In Venice, we toured the Doge's Palace, climbing flight after flight of uneven stairs. We were baffled to find ourselves exiting on ground level.

The Vatican's "shorter" hike to the Sistine Chapel includes stairs up, stairs down, and random inclines, culminating in a five-story curling ramp. Add in uneven cobblestone streets and I found port days exhausting on my own two feet. Attempting that in a wheelchair or scooter would have been simply impossible.

Some tours are a challenge as well. Clambering around ancient ruins, over sandy trails, up and down mountains, over jungle canopies on zip lines, rocky paths, walking on glaciers, etc, may well be infeasible. Getting in and out of a tour bus or van may prove difficult, too. Rather than missing out, do your due research and plan activities you can participate in, not just as a spectator. This is yet another reason to book private tours. A big bus may not be able to accommodate a wheel chair, but once you're comfortably seated in a van, you're good to go.

Bottom line: ask a lot of questions, of the cruise line, the ship itself, and any tour guides you may hire. And plan on being flexible; you really have no choice.

Ship Excursions, Private Tours, or Wing It?

I have a fear of Missing Something Wonderful. That's why I read up on any place we visit. I'm eager to see and do as much as possible in the time I'm *anywhere* new, figuring I may never get back there again. The Cruise Addict and I like to book private tours in most ports. I calculate we save 45%-65% over a ship-sponsored tour, and we see much more, while having the flexibility to do exactly what we want. Plus, I'm not a fan of crowds, and most ships' tours are on buses, which is like packing your very own crowd with you, all day. I like private tours!

Forget the cattle calls and packed coach (bus!) tours; savvy cruisers know that hiring a private tour guide is often the best way to visit a port of call. The cruise lines don't like to hear it (a huge profit on cruises comes from shore excursions) but the advantages of going it on your own are numerous. You can set a personalized itinerary, travel in a smaller group and see the sights at your own speed. And while you could get carried away and spend a fortune, we've always saved money going on our own.

The cruise lines push hard for their shore excursions, and they're not all bad. They're okay if you're a fearful traveler who likes being herded in a nice, safe group rather than seeing and doing more in a new place. Personally, the only times I've found them useful is as an airport transfer in the destination city. Those take your luggage, give an overview-type tour of the city, and end at the airport. You don't have to wrangle luggage, and it eats up time you'd otherwise have spent staring at the wall at Gate 34 A. Plus, you might learn something. The one we took in Boston visited five places we missed on our own. Granted, I was fine not seeing Fenway Park, but the statues were interesting.

On Your Own

Having done your research at home, you may well find you don't need a tour at all. Don't bother with a live tour guide when main attractions are easily accessible. You can skip a tour if you know where you're going, too; such as Fort Adams in Newport, RI, or The Freedom Trail in Boston. You surely don't need a tour to find the Point Roberts tram in Juneau; it's visible from the ship.

To plot your day, try http://www.tomsportguides.com/, tripadvisor.com, or do an online search for the city's name, and "tourism." You might even add in "free things to do," or "nightlife" or "festivals" if that appeals to you. You can often find museums, restaurants, parks, incredible sites you had no idea existed, within walking distance or an easy cab ride away. We've had great success with that, in ports right near an interesting city. Some places are best gone *through*, not *to*. Read up to see if your cruise ports in a good place, or an industrial port in a sketchy region.

In Toulon, France, we knew there was a Sunday market, a fine Maritime museum (the area is rich in history), a beautiful beach, and Le Petit Train that left from the port and gave a good overview of the city. That, combined with some wandering, the best éclair I've ever eaten, and an outdoor restaurant with free Wi-Fi to check on the kids at home, made for a perfectly relaxing day in the south of France. After eleven intensive port days, it was just what we needed.

In your planning, I suggest seek out cheap and free things to do in any port. Any place labeled Old Town is guaranteed to have interesting things. I like visitors' centers; they're a microcosm of local lore and history, neatly condensed. Local parks are often fun, as are quirky little shops. Window shopping costs nothing, contrary to Husband's claims. While you're browsing, ask the clerk what they recommend you see next. Best fudge on the planet, free gold panning, a local fossil field open to the public? What are you waiting for?

National Park Service walking tours are free, available in quite a few US ports, and interesting. We learned about Soapy Smith in Skagway, Alaska, from a ranger who was a master storyteller. Soapy was a skilled con artist, bent on fleecing homesick gold miners. Mining the gold miners for gold, as it were. Among other creative schemes, Soapy demanded outrageous fees for the use of his exclusive telegraph to send a few words to loved ones back home. The catch; his telegraph operator dutifully keyed in the precious messages, but the telegraph line never left the building. Bonus: if his men caught messages about miners hitting pay dirt, Soapy's crew paid a visit to the claim, post-haste, and not for a tea party.

In Boston, we missed the paid walking tour I wanted by fifteen minutes. A passer-by recommended the free tour by the National Park Service, starting in a few minutes. That led to some of my best memories of Boston. I know for a fact the guide covered more Revolutionary War history than anyone else could have, and better, too. She had us laughing, then choked up, awed as she painted a living picture of the events that shaped America's history, right where we walked. She asserted, "Philadelphia is known as the birthplace of America, but Boston was the labor room, where the real work took place."

Ask a local or a staff member, "What's the port known for?" Rather than buying dust-catchers sold in souvenir shops, aim for something meaningful or delicious. Mexican vanilla, Caribbean Essence or jerk seasoning, a lobster cookie cutter from Maine, a luscious scarf from Istanbul, a photo wall calendar from Venice; choose something memorable.

Look for souvenirs and experiences in unusual places. Grocery stores are a wonderful way to get a sense of how people live day-to-day. And you may find genuine, inexpensive souvenirs there. Pharmacies, fabric stores, and hardware stores are also really interesting. Find out what's made locally, what the area is known for. Fabric in Samoa, silver in Barbados, marbled paper in Italy, muskox yarn from Alaska, all wrapped in a memory, are the best. Items you can't find anywhere else make wonderful treasures.

If you plan a full day onshore, as opposed to the lazy-sit-around variety, look into a city pass. You can buy them online. We've found them in most major cities, and they can save you a bundle! In some cases, they cost less than a single ship's shore excursion, letting you experience much, much more. Let me show you some examples.

City Pass Seattle includes seven major venues: zoo, Space Needle, Pacific Science Center, even a harbor boat tour. In Stockholm, the city pass covers *sixty* attractions for one low price: Wasa Museum, the Royal Palace and stables, Tivoli amusement park, the state cathedral with the gold

statue of King George slaying the dragon, even a Hop On Hop
Off tour and a guided walking tour of the Old City. The
HOHO is by boat, not bus; Stockholm sits on eight islands.
Seeing the Wasa alone is well worth the price. It's a museum
built around a full sized ship that sank twenty *minutes* into its
first sailing, right in the harbor, in 1628. The muck and cold
water preserved it remarkably well. It was recovered, whole,
in 1961. It's a stunning feeling to stand inches from a
perfectly preserved ship from that long ago.

Miami's City Pass covers entry to twenty attractions,
from a sightseeing cruise to a duck tour to a bike rental, even
the zoo, ensuring any activity level will find great things to
do. In Los Angeles, the pass covers over twenty attractions,
including Madame Tussaud's, tours of the star's
neighborhoods, a VIP studio tour, La Brea Tar Pits, even
Knott's Berry Farm, rolled into one low price.

We've also had great luck with ubiquitous guy-with-
a-sign tours in places we intended to explore on our own. In
Puerto Rico, we intended to take a cab to the forts, then walk
around the Old Square. Twenty feet from the pier, Husband
was snagged by a man waving a poster, touting the wonderful
two hour tour for $20, total. Husband's eyes lit up. We found
ourselves in a small van with ten of our new best friends, and
it turned out to be a good experience.

As he drove to the capitol, the driver told us about life
on the island. He said the cabbies and tour drivers all gather
every morning to chat and pray. "All day, we fight each other
for customers, but in the morning, we pray."

Elderly residents are highly respected in Puerto Rico.
After age 65, tickets to museums, shows, movies, etc., are half

price, along with all restaurant meals. After age 70, they're free, and they no longer pay property taxes! Don't call your real estate agent. You have to live there ten years before those benefits kick in.

Grandma, he said, rules the family. "Her word is law; no one speaks after Grandma has her say. And no one hurts or even interrupts an old person. If you hurt an old one, you're gonna get beat up, *bad.*"

Across the street from the stately capitol building, I noticed a row of nine life-sized bronze statues of US presidents. Nine?

I asked, "Where are the others?"

Our guide explained those were to honor those presidents who came to San Juan during their presidency. "You show up, we make a statue. You don't care enough to come see us, you get nothing."

That surprised me; a president has four, or maybe eight, years in office, yet they couldn't make the trip? Who was it that said showing up is half the battle?

Private Tours

In Europe, most city centers ban vehicles over twelve passengers. That means your lovely bus tour will drop you off out of the area, requiring up to a 45-minute hike before you even reach the site you wish to see. By the time you straggle in, our little private van has let us off us at the doorstep, we've seen the place, had lunch, and we're on our way out, with energy to spare.

Book tours through a local company or ask your travel agent to arrange a private tour. Reserve them well before you set sail; good ones fill up fast. It's easier than you think! Last year, I arranged ten tours in ten ports in five countries, back to back, from my own computer. I had to factor in time zones, but email was easy—I never even made a phone call. Each was an incredible experience.

I've had great luck by simply googling 'shore excursion Saint John' or whatever port you're looking at. Typing 'tour,' or 'day tour' also works, but specifying 'shore excursion' narrows the field to companies accustomed to working with cruise passengers' time constraints. It also eliminates the awkward need to make your way to the pick-up point, often at a hotel somewhere. Tours labeled 'shore excursion' automatically pick up and drop off right at the port, saving you time, plus the cost of a taxi or two.

A tour you arrange yourself has so many advantages! Do some research and find private guides so that you can do exactly what you want to do. I'm convinced it's the best way to see as much as possible in a new place in the shortest amount of time. In Italy, we took a private tour. Our driver met us at the pier, and drove us to Pisa, telling stories about the US military base on the way. We had plenty of time in Pisa, then drove to Florence, passing sunflower fields. He stopped at a city overlook and had us so enthralled with stories about the place and its history, we almost took root, right there.

After a wonderful tour of Florence, we ate lunch in a place where I doubted any tourist had set foot. Our guide introduced me to a paper-seller who made the hand crafted marbled paper the area is known for. Tired after two weeks of travel, we opted to skip yet another museum. Instead, Giovanni turned uphill, into the Tuscany of postcards, with rolling hills lined with dusky olive trees and Chantilly grapes nearing harvest. The day was magical, guided by a local resident, full of stories. Our friends took a local train to Pisa, climbed the tower, and returned to the ship. Same amount of time spent.

In Citivecchia, 90 minutes from Rome, we took another private tour. As we stepped off the ship, I overheard a couple of passengers muse, "It's our first time here. What is there to do?" Are you *kidding* me? All I could do was shake my head.

We spotted our guide, waving a name card for us at the bottom of the gangway, and off we went. Our first stop was Saint Paul's Basilica, a towering golden cathedral where (part of) Paul is buried. We walked through the city square. Our guide handed us advance tickets to the Vatican Museo and Sistine Chapel. Did you know the museum's s*hort* route to the Sistine Chapel is 4.77 *miles* long? Artwork overload! Next we stopped in St. Peter's Square, and admired the pope's balcony and living quarters (from outside; he was not at home). The Pantheon was next–I couldn't believe I was really there! On to the Seven Hills of Rome, including the spot where the madman, Nero, played his fiddle in the last hours as civilization burned around him. The ruins were awesome; I live in a very young country.

Across the way stood Rome's Coliseum, incongruously surrounded by frenetic traffic whizzing past. We went inside the Coliseum, avoiding the plastic-clad gladiators posing for expensive photo ops. Our tour guide took us to lunch and pastry by Piazza Navona's elaborate fountain, where I bought a lovely windowpane wrap. Trevi Fountain was closed for construction; he assured us throwing a coin in any fountain would ensure our return. Our leisurely drive back to the ship was full of stories about the area and people. Delightful day!

Back on the ship, I happened to be in an elevator with the same people I'd overheard nine hours earlier. They'd walked to a coffee house they saw from the ship, then came back onboard, bored, having no idea of what all they'd missed. If nothing else, they were within mere blocks of an active archeological dig, where an ancient Roman ship, fully loaded, had been unearthed the previous month! I marvel at how people can be somewhere, yet have no idea where they are.

Private tour guides work best in ports where it's difficult to get to certain places, or in destinations where you'd like to do a specific activity or see a *lot* in the time you have. Think along the lines of a driver for the twisty highways of Italy's Amalfi Coast or an expert in cheeses for a tour of Parma's namesake dairies. A private tour guide can also give you an excellent overview of an island, particularly if you'd rather go in a smaller vehicle than a bus.

Cosol Tours in St Lucia made for a delightful day trip. We covered most of the island, had lunch at a private home, stopped at a resort to swim, took in the worlds' only drive-in volcano, stopped for warm bread and local cheese, toured a banana plantation, and sampled the local drinks all day. Those bananas were like none I've ever eaten before! So sweet, warm from the sun, they were almost creamy, like a whole different fruit. Husband detests bananas; I was sad to see him gobble his up. Private drivers can be hired in most ports in the Caribbean on the spot; preplanning is nice, but not required.

Another advantage of private tours is the cost. It's by the vehicle, not per person. A $400 tour sounds expensive, until you divide that by eight (people), and divide *that* by six (hours), and realize the cost includes tickets to four sites for all of you ... that's not much at all, per person!

If your party is not large enough to fill a van, ask the tour company to hook you up; there may well be a partially full tour, just waiting for you. Or ask on an online roll call (Cruisecritic.com's roll calls are great for this). Cruisers on your same ship will likely jump at the chance to split costs and have a fabulous tour. We did this again in Gibraltar; never laid eyes on the other people until that morning, but we automatically had a lot in common.

Once you've narrowed your search down to several potential tour guides, start sending emails. In your initial contact, you'll want to state the date that you'll be in port, how many people are in your party and tell them what kind of tour you are looking for. For example, "It's our first time in Izmir, we want to see as much as we can, we're not interested in a long lunch break or a rug factory, there are nine of us ranging in age from teen to retired, we need an English-speaking guide, and we'll be on the Gemini Crudo on September 7th."

Guides also often have set tours, which you can customize, within reason. If you really want to see La Brea

Tar Pits, the confluence of the Columbia River, or the
cemetery where the Titanic victims lie, speak up, ahead of
time if you can. Make sure to tell them the hours that your
ship will be in port. Tour companies deal with cruise
passengers all the time, and they know getting you back on
time is critical to their livelihood. You have the power to
write a review online, and they know their future business
depends on you writing a positive one!

Your correspondence with your guide doesn't end
with the booking. Once you narrow your options down to one
tour company, go ahead and put down a deposit if required,
using a secure website. Not all require a deposit, and most
tours want payment at the end of the tour day, not ahead of
time. You'll want to make sure you have your contract in
writing. Double check the itinerary, making changes as
needed. In Ephesus, it's common to stop at the House of
Mary, but our friends were more interested in the Terraced
Houses. Our guide not only agreed to the change, but even
paid the extra entrance fee.

As your cruise draws closer, the tour guide should
email you to confirm the tour and give you instructions on
where and when to meet. Most private guides will greet you
with a sign bearing your name right at the pier; if they're not
permitted inside the gates, make sure you understand exactly
where to meet. Take the company's phone number onshore,
just in case.

Don't forget about advance entry tickets to attractions.
Most private tours suggest them, many require them, others
provide them as part of the price. An advance ticket can save
money, but more importantly, reserving tickets for a specific
time allows you to skip the line waiting to get in, and

guarantees the venue will be available that day for you. Some attractions limit the number of visitors in any hour. You could squander an afternoon just waiting for a spot to open up. They're the best use of time, trust me.

In several places, I felt almost guilty waltzing past hundreds of people in line, walking right in the front door like a VIP, when all I did was reserve a ticket online weeks ahead of time. *Almost* guilty; not quite ... More like smart.

Enjoy the Flexibility

One of the best things about having a private guide is that you aren't hampered by set times and schedules. Having done your homework, you'll have a good idea of what you'd like to do and see that day, but you don't know as much as a local resident. If your guide suggests a jaunt to the top of Mount Vesuvius, a stop at a marvelous bakery with more kinds of baklava than you knew existed, or offers to show you the very steps where Julius Caesar was murdered (stabbed thirty-two times!), be flexible.

Conversely, if you want more time at the Coliseum, or are bored at yet another "Genuine Ancient Roman Coin" stand, speak up. If time allows, most are very willing to make adjustments.

Don't forget the tip. Keep in mind that guides' livelihood depends on tips from tourists. Plan on at least 10-15%; more if the tour was outstanding. Some of our tour guides have been so wonderful, we've tipped much more.

What to Wear on a Cruise

Yes, of course, it's your vacation; you've earned it, you've planned for it, and you deserve it. The thing is, so did every other person on the ship. In dress, as in everything else, please be considerate of others. You may be able to push the dress code without verbal repercussions, but no one wants to see your hairy armpits in the dining room. No one *really* wants to see what gets displayed when you bend over in those too-short short shorts, sans undies. Trust me; you may insist you're comfortable, but you'd be a lot less so if you knew what people were thinking about you.

Simply put, every place you go has a dress code, implied or stated. You wouldn't wear a ball gown to the beach, and you shouldn't wear a sweaty work out outfit to a nice restaurant. Keep in mind some places are more formal than others. In America, you're fine wearing jeans and tees most places; in Europe, resort-casual is best. In Bermuda, even the golf courses have strict dress codes. Some other cruise itineraries, such as Hawaii, the Mexican Riviera, the Caribbean, and French Polynesia are more casual than the norm. Where else can you get away with wearing brightly flowered Aloha shirts in public?

If you're visiting religious sites in the Middle East or some parts of Europe, some sites request covered shoulders and knees covered, for both genders, even if it's quite hot. Yes, you may disagree. You may also be barred from entering if you don't comply.

At Istanbul's Blue Mosque, men and women are required to cover legs and remove their shoes, and women must also cover their hair, neck, and arms. I felt close to fainting from lack of air with the provided big headscarf twined around my neck and hair. It wasn't much better once I twisted it up on top of my head, like a towel after I wash my curls. One young woman in our group handled the situation more gracefully: she simply flipped up the hood on her sweatshirt. Planning ahead is a good idea!

Keep in mind Europe is dressier than America, overall. Dressing too casually (tank tops, scruffy jeans, any kind of athletic garb) is considered disrespectful in many ports of call. And you know it's true: a person in nice clothes is likely to be more warmly welcomed in restaurants and shops than the guy who looks like he walked away from a car repair job. True, you may never see those people again, but you might as well leave a good impression the first time. On active shore excursions or beach days, ultra-casual is just fine.

Daytime on cruise ships calls for casual clothing, but please keep it decent. Short shorts are best kept to the pool deck or the fitness center. Wearing them to lunch in the buffet is stretching it. Bathing suits are only appropriate at the pool; coming and going, please wear a cover up or shirt so folks in a crowded elevator aren't more intimate than either of you would like. Appropriate cover-ups are fine for lunching at the poolside grill or buffet. Bare feet are a good idea only pool-side. Those pretty tile floors are treacherous when wet.

Cruise ships assign daily dress codes – casual, informal, resort casual, formal– that take effect in public rooms and restaurants from about 6 p.m. onward. On most seven-night cruises, you can plan on two formal nights, a couple of casual evenings and a handful of dressy nights. Of course this varies by cruise lines, so read before you go.

Many people look forward to formal nights; when else do you get to don bowtie and sequins? If you're opposed to anything dressier than shorts, don't worry. You may not be allowed in the main dining room, specialty restaurants, or shows on some lines, but you can always eat in the buffet or order room service. On other cruise lines, the dress code is "suggested," not required.

Men can pack a tuxedo, but tuxes are increasingly being outnumbered by business-suit-and-tie on formal nights. On some ships, you can rent tuxedos, if you want one for an elegant photo shoot. On all but the most casual ships, I'd recommend men pack at least a collared shirt, tie, and nice trousers. In some onboard specialty restaurants, you'd feel out of place in anything less.

On dress-up night, you'll see more cocktail dresses than formal gowns on all but the most prim and proper ships. Women don't need silk ball gowns (whew!) anymore. On the other hand, go ahead and bring it if you'd like, along with that fluffy bridesmaid dress hanging in the closet. Now's your chance to wear it one more time.

The current trend towards maxi skirts is great for cruising. They're made of fabrics you can wad in a suitcase without wrinkling, dressy enough to tour cathedrals, you can wear them over a swimsuit to the beach, and they look fine for any dinner. You'll look at least as good as everyone else, and better than most. Bonus: they're among the most comfortable items you can wear, short of pajamas. Please don't wear those in public. Thank you.

Male or female, go with the layered look. A light sweater or sweatshirt will ward off the aggressive air conditioning or chilly afternoon. Alaska cruisers most likely need everything from bathing suits and short-sleeve tops to warm fleece jackets, hats and gloves for Glacier Day; the same goes for cruising round the Horn of South America, where weather can vary 40 degrees in a day. Layers work better than a single too-bulky item.

You may want to pack a hat to protect against the sun or keep your ears warm during scenic glacier or fjord cruising. I was glad I'd thrown my wide brimmed hat in when I clambered over ancient ruins in Turkey. Besides the hot sun beating down, the old stones reflected it back up; effectively cooking both sides. The floppy hat helped! Our family album includes a lovely photo of me sunbathing on a lounge chair in Glacier Bay, bundled up with only my eyes showing. Yes, I looked silly, but without that woolly hat, I'd have had to retreat indoors, and what fun is that?

Try not to pack a suitcase full of shoes. I've seen it done. Flip-flops are fine for a beach day, but you'll want more structured shoes for long days of sightseeing. Closed-toe shoes are required for zip lines, and smart for rocky hikes up to Juneau's abandoned gold mine. Cushy, light shoes will let you enjoy long days touring. Don't wear the brand new stiff ones ... a little blister can ruin your day. For most cruises, three pair of shoes is enough; sneakers, a fairly dressy pair, and sandals or water shoes if you know you'll hit a rocky beach on your cruise.

Regardless of how many you pack, bring multi-purpose footwear, such as sneakers that go from gym to sightseeing, or strappy sandals that'll do by the pool and at dinner. You can probably get by with less-than-perfectly-color-coordinated dress shoes. My motto: if you can't match, contrast. The old fashion-police rules are out the window, unless you have a teen aged daughter.

You may still run into judgmental dunderheads who consider *your* attire *their* business. Sorry about that. My own mother was laughed at in an elevator onboard for wearing Sketchers with her formal dress. Had the man known she had broken her toe the previous day when the ship's bookshelf fell on her foot, perhaps he would have understood those were the only shoes that fit. Nah; people who mock strangers in public are clueless.

What to Pack

As you pack, figure out what you'll need, then bring it. Common sense, right? I told my kids over the years, "Think about what you'll be doing, and dress appropriately." Once our kids were about two or three years old, they did their own packing, with minimal guidance. I'd draw a little sketch of the item they needed, and how many of each, then they'd choose from that category: shirts, swimsuit, jammies. Usually, my sketches were close enough to guess. Once in a while, they'd ask, "Mommy, why do I need a fish?" I'm not good at drawing socks.

You can easily find dozens of packing lists online, most of which will see you through just about anything. I'm not going to tell you how to pack, beyond a few suggestions. Let's see if I can do this in fifteen.

Suggestion #1:

Make a packing list if you need one. It's not a character flaw to write stuff down so you'll remember it, contrary to what Husband believes. I have a rough packing list, and he does not. Want to guess which one of us needed to stop at a store to buy razors and antiperspirant on the way to *three cruises in a row*? Need a hint? It was the guy with the fluffy mustache.

On the third time, I suggested he just buy antiperspirant on the ship; enough, already! He balked, saying the brand they stock feels like a glue stick, and he didn't like the Velcro-tearing sensation every time he lifted his arm.

"How do you know that?"

"I forgot it last year, too."

Suggestion #2

Pack your <u>carry-on bag</u> thoughtfully. Once you check your luggage at the cruise terminal, you won't see the bags again for hours. If you plan to hit the hot tub, bring your bathing suit. If you plan to hit the buffet, bring your dentures. If you have small children, make sure you have enough diapers to get you through most of the day. Whatever you'll need for the first half of the day, stick it in your carry-on bag. The Guest Services desk won't even listen to you complain about lost bags until after dinner. Plan ahead, or you could be Those People who wear a Detroit sweatshirt in Miami, since that's what they needed on the flight from home. And don't forget to add in your medicines and camera!

Suggestion #3

<u>Don't over pack.</u> Most packing lists expect you to bring enough to outfit every passenger on your deck.

My style is to think through each day, each possible scenario for your trip. What activities will I be doing, and do I have something to wear for each possibility? Swimsuit, parka, sequined blouse, shorts? Add in a few wraps, against either chilly weather or aggressive air conditioning, and some comfy shoes, and I'm all set. Oh, I try to ensure each item can mix-and-match at least three different ways. I've seen passengers boarding for a five day cruise with three bulging suitcases each. Unless you're changing wardrobe every hour on the hour, that's probably too much. My rule: don't pack more than you can wrangle yourself. The days of ladies' maids are past.

Suggestion #4

Don't under pack, either. It's perfectly fine to wear the same outfit twice, unless you spilled soup on it the first time. Yes, you can wear the same outfit to dinner every night on a twelve-day cruise, but why would you? Online, you can find packing lists on what to bring for a 21-day cruise that'll all fit in your briefcase. I've met those people, going on a two week vacation with just a carry on.

Suit yourself; I don't do that. I crave light and color and variety. At home, I often change clothes a couple of times a day. I couldn't face that navy blue blouse one more day, even if it had a soft yellow scarf to jazz it up. I technically over pack; there; I admit it. So long as I don't ask you to carry it, you don't get a vote on the subject.

Some people recommend packing old, raggedy items to jettison along the way. I feel better in a favorite shirt, a blouse I look good in, nice pants. I'm on vacation– I pack things that make me happy.

Suggestion #5:

Regardless of how much you end up packing, <u>keep weight in mind</u>. The luggage, not yourself. Khakis and breezy cottons are much lighter than jeans, and dry faster, should they get wet. Plus, you can dress them up or down with various shirts, making them suitable just about anywhere short of formal night.

Suggestion #6:

<u>Leave some room in your luggage</u>. If you have to sit on the suitcase at home to close it, that's too much stuff. Save space for at least a few souvenirs during your cruise. Whether you're picking up leather goods in Italy, Aloha-wear in Hawaii, or duty-free goods in the Caribbean, consider packing a foldable duffle. It won't take up much space in your suitcase. If you buy more than you expected (some deals are too great to walk past!), you can check it or call it a second carry on on the flight home. If the weather catches you off guard, you can almost always buy a sweater or dry shirt or rain poncho at your destination.

Suggestion #7:

<u>Consider the weather,</u> which can turn on a dime. I overheard a man in Glacier Bay berating a crew member because he was chilly, as if that was her fault. All he had packed was shorts and tees, because "Everybody knows cruises are warm." On that same cruise, we met a woman

frantically shopping while fanning herself in Ketchikan's unusual 85 degree heatwave. She'd only brought bulky sweaters, secure in her knowledge that Alaska is always cold.

I don't care what the forecast says – the meteorologist wasn't referring to the middle of the ocean when he said it would be 80 degrees. It gets cold and windy out there in the open! I recommend layers, which you can add to or remove as needed Bring a jacket, or at least a windbreaker, so you're not stuck below decks. Pashminas and wraps are a stylish defense against chill winds and breezy air conditioning. Forgot yours? Every ship I've seen sells them; call it a souvenir.

Suggestion #8

Party on, if that's your thing. Check your cruise's itinerary before you pack, and read a few recent cruise reviews, too. Many cruise lines have a theme party one night, maybe 50s, Hawaiian luau, pirates, or NCL's white hot parties. Hit the local dollar store near home for costume accessories; grass skirts, coconut bras, plastic swords, goofy glasses, etc, all fit nicely, cost little, and will jazz up your evening onboard.

Suggestion # 9

It's up to you to have the documents you require at hand. On just about every cruise I've taken, a handful of passengers become spectators, watching the ship sail without them because they didn't have the proper papers. It's up to you to have a passport, visa if required, etc, along with the cruise boarding documents, preferably filled out on line ahead of time, and in your hand as well. Have your wallet with a credit card handy at check in, too. It's up to you to verify what you need. Don't count on the cruise line to tell you. This isn't really a suggestion: more like a decree. If you want to get on the ship, jump the required hoops.

Suggestion #10

Pack whatever personal items you need for comfort on the cruise, including extra glasses/reading glasses/sunglasses. Did I tell you about the time Husband forgot to remove his glasses at Orient Beach? Luckily, I was able to spot them underwater, after a wave knocked them off his face. I did hesitate to hand them over. At a Clothing Optional beach, perhaps he was better off blurry.

Suggestion #11

Pack a journal or notebook for making notes. Once you're back home after a whirlwind cruise, it's easy to forget which was the Parthenon and which the Pantheon. And was what that savory spice you're going to look for at home? Met someone interesting? You'll want their contact info. Trust me; write it down.

Suggestion #12

Pack your can't-live-without-it electronics: cell phone, tablet, laptop, etc, and their chargers. If you're planning to work out, pack your iPod or mp3 player to stave off boredom on the treadmill. Bring a camera, and consider a disposable underwater camera for snorkeling or beach days, plus extra memory cards. I label my photos by the day, in photo-intensive places. Or, start each day by taking a quick shot of the elevator's floor, where the day of the week is displayed.

I also bring a small travel alarm clock. Ship's current can vary widely, causing a plug-in clock to run fast, or slow, or both in the same afternoon. Battery operated is better. Toss in a slim flashlight, in case of power outages. I've been told I worry about things that never happen. How do you know the reason they didn't happen *because* I put thought into it, hmm?

Suggestion # 13:

You don't need a full-size pharmacy unless you're going to the North Pole, but do bring your prescription drugs and any other essential medications you might want along the way. I buy over-the-counter medicine at the dollar store. The smaller packages take less space than full size bottles, and I probably won't have a headache requiring a Costco-sized bottle on a cruise. Or anywhere else, for that matter. A list of your current meds is smart, in case a random doctor asks. It's best to pack these in your carry-on bag. Luggage is rarely lost, but let's not tempt fate, shall we?

I also bring a small first aid-type kit, including band aids, antacids, anti-itch/antibiotic cream, anti-diarrhea medication, cough drops, aspirin/anti-inflammatory meds, etc. Mine fits in a quart-size zip-type bag easily.

Bring bug repellant, if your destinations are summery, especially if you're going somewhere on the Zika watch list.

Jungle tours are more enjoyable if you're not the bug's picnic basket. Oh, and don't forget sunscreen, and aloe lotion for the places you neglect to apply sunscreen. The sun closer to the equator is much hotter than you're used to, and you're more likely to be outdoors more than at home on any cruise, unless your day job is a groundskeeper. It's easy to forget to reapply sunblock when you're enjoying snorkeling. A sunburned back can make you miserable.

Past-dated sunscreen is likely ineffective. We learned that when Daughter applied it liberally in the Caribbean, and still looked like a sad cooked lobster by dinner. Read the expiration date; it's cheap insurance.

Suggestion # 14

Unless you've booked a top-shelf cruise line, or a fancy mega-suite, your luggage tags are no longer mailed to you, already filled out. Sad, huh? You'll need to print them out yourself. Print them at home, but don't attach them on the luggage until you reach the port, or just before. Airlines confuse easily as it is, without your help.

If you forget to grab your tags, don't have a come-apart. You can always pick up blank ones at the port. Fill it out yourself; the porters are too busy to worry about tidy penmanship on turn-around day. Write neatly. Several times, we've had other peoples' bags delivered to our cabin because their 8 looked like a 2.

My favorite travel agent gave us a pile of plastic sleeves that slip onto the luggage handles. Versions are available to buy online. Some passengers print tags on cardstock, or have them laminated at a copy shop. You can also reinforce them yourself with a strip of clear packing tape. A mini-stapler, a twist-tie, or a panduit is great to secure them to each suitcase. Off you go!

Whatever method you use, I recommend attaching *two* luggage tags to each bag, one on the top, one on the side, in case one gets torn off. On every embarkation day, the dock and hallways end up littered with tags. Have pity on the crew; make it easy for them to be delivered straight to your cabin.

Suggestion # 15

Pack easy-care clothing. Comfortable knits and synthetics pack well, although natural fabrics are cooler. Not linen; I can wrinkle linen just by looking at it. Thin plastic sheets between clothes lessen wrinkles in clothing in the suitcases. You can use drycleaner plastic, large trash bags, or even tissue paper between layers.

Some savvy cruisers pack their clothing in a trash bag inside the suitcases, especially if they have soft-sided luggage and rain is forecast. The tropics, especially, have sudden, drenching rains, not like the Northwest, where it drizzles for eight months and drips off the trees the rest of the year. On very rare occasions, luggage loaded into the bins to transport onto ship by crane have been dropped into the drink. Trash bags are not a bad idea!

Plain tap water in a refillable spray bottle works great for taking out wrinkles in clothing. Pack a cheap plant-mister type bottle empty and fill it on arrival, thereby reducing the weight to essentially nothing. Just spray the wrinkles, give the shirt a shake, smooth out the collar and placket and hang it up. Or, just put it on. Your body heat will dry it in minutes. No worries about leakage in your suitcase and no odor, either. We've use this method for years.

On our first cruise, we traveled with another couple. Every afternoon, she'd excuse herself to go iron her husband's shirt for dinner. I was aghast! In the first place; he was an adult, and capable of ironing his own darn shirt. In the second place, she was a bad example. The 1940's are past, where they belong!

Other Items to Pack

A friend asked what random items I pack, then exclaimed, "How ever do you manage? I couldn't fit all that in my suitcase!" Silly; besides clothing and electronics, my Other category fits easily in a large zip-type bag, with plenty of room to squish air out. It stays assembled, ready to grab at a minute's notice. I live with The Cruise Addict, who starts most days by asking, "Can I book a cruise today? If I find a great deal, then can I?" I can pack in under twenty minutes, if the laundry is caught up at the time.

A night light can save your shins in a dark cabin. If you don't want anything that bright, get a few glow sticks, one per night. They last about eight hours. Loop one over a doorknob or set on the cabin's floor to provide just enough light to reach the bathroom in the dark. Some cruise ships have a light in the closet that leaks enough to be a fine nightlight, but don't count on your cabin having one.

Ear plugs can prevent rage on a cruise ship. You can pick up a pair at Guest Services, but the ones you buy at home might be more comfortable. Setting aside in-cabin sounds, such as a haunted bathroom and your cabin mate's snoring, those stateroom walls can sound paper thin. I'm sure your next door neighbor had no idea you didn't want to listen to *Star Wars* at full volume at four o'clock in the morning. Nor did the crew consider how high you'd jump when they drop anchor before dawn. Earplugs will help you sleep better, without the murderous instincts that accompany such rude awakenings.

Bring binoculars, or opera glasses. You'll use these to hunt for bears and whales, and admire the waterfall and ruins. They're also handy for seeing intricate indoor details, such as the frieze in that cathedral's tall ceiling.

I pack a small zip-type bag of 'office supplies' on every cruise. Magnets to hold assorted papers to the cabin walls, paperclips, clothespins, highlighter for the daily schedule, markers for notes and labeling items, pens, 3 X 5 cards, sticky notes for messages to cabin steward and traveling companions, clear tape, duct tape, and a pair of child size scissors all take up little space, and come in handy. I also pack super glue, every cruise. I've used it to repair a broken nail, necklace link and tote bag clasp, to mention a few uses.

Small quantities of tape, wrapped around a marker or other item you're bringing is a good idea. From fixing a torn hem to securing an abused suitcase, duct tape is indispensable. Don't use it to hold drawers shut in a storm. Blue painter's tape is gentler on surfaces. You don't want to pay to refinish that dresser when all is said and done.

Some cruise lines no longer provide pens in cabins; I always have pen and small paper at hand. Have you seen the Facebook meme that says, "I'm an author. Be nice to me, or you'll end up in my next book"? Humor is always based in fact. You never know when a character onboard can morph into character in a story. For non-writers, it's handy to be able to jot down that great idea you overheard.

At home, I use wooden spring-type clothespins all over the house, for clamping chips bags in the pantry, hanging dainties to dry overnight, securing notes/papers/lists/checks for errand-running, pinching curtains open (or closed), corralling electrical cords under my desk, on and on. I bought a 50-pack from a dollar store about ten years ago, and haven't gone through them all yet. They're a bargain. On cruise ships, clips are great for holding curtains in place, draping wet suits on the in-shower clothesline, keeping your kid's socks from migrating, as well as clipping papers together. I don't know why papers multiply on cruise ships, but they do.

A small sewing kit comes in handy. I made mine by threading a length of neutral dark and light threads on two hand-sewing needles, wrapped around a two-inch square cardboard. Add a few safety pins, and four buttons (two light, two dark), and there you go. Nail clippers can double as scissors for snipping threads. If you're not good at sewing, pack some double stick tape to hold up your torn hem, and duct tape for mending just about anything else. You're on your own if you pop a button.

Zip-type plastic bags have many uses, such as packing any toiletries that might leak, corralling dirty and wet things, packing snacks for your shore excursion, as a souvenir- and camera-protector, kid-clothes organizer, barf bags, keeping brochures together, used-diaper holders until you can find a trash bin ... On every trip, I find another use for them!

People tend to forget their jewelry, credit cards, or watches in the safe when they leave. I keep our valuables inside a zip-type plastic bag inside the safe. It's easy to grab everything all at once, and the small stuff has no chance to escape to the dark recesses. You don't want to get halfway home and notice you forgot your travel documents or favorite necklace.

We bring a couple small games to play on the deck, balcony, or game room. A deck of cards is small and the games you can devise with it are endless. A cruiser pulled out a pack of travel-size lightweight dominoes, and had a game of Mexican Train going in no time. If you need a partner for Canasta, just ask; many people would love a game.

What *Not* to Pack on a Cruise

A pretty red swimsuit's label read Dry Clean Only. Those penguin potholders were labeled Do Not Expose To Heat. Hairdryers plainly caution Do Not Use In Bathtub Or Shower. I'm all about efficiency, but how on earth could a person even think about drying their hair *while* washing it? Like the crazy labels I've seen on items, I sometimes wonder why the rules are in place on ships. At some point, did enough people bring popcorn poppers onboard cruise ships to require a policy in writing?

Besides not bringing your million dollar bracelet and favorite 72" TV, there are some items that are flat-out forbidden on a cruise ship. Some are for safety reasons, some are not allowed because ... no one knows why. Just go with it.

These items will be confiscated it they're found (and they're nearly always found):

Popcorn poppers

Pots and pans

Rice cookers

Power strips (the ones with cords; the plug-type are okay)

Irons

Hot plates/convection burners

Toasters

Electric coffee pots and tea kettles

Electric pressure cookers

Microwave ovens (the ship provides food, you know)

Barbecue grills

Candles *Battery operated candles are allowed, and create a nice ambiance. Do not use them on your balcony! Once we heard a "Bravo, Bravo, Bravo" announcement: FIRE! Turns out staff on the bridge saw an open flame on a balcony, and sent out the alert. Firefighter teams arrived in full gear, and found a couple enjoying wine by the light of a battery-operated candle. So much for a lovely romantic evening. The rule: If you can see the bridge, they can see you.*

Incense

Travel steamers

Heating pads

Flammable liquids and dangerous chemicals. *Even if you're a famous oil painter, a ship is not the place for turpentine.*

Firearms & ammunition, including realistic replicas. *Leave your battle axe collection at home, in other words.*

161

Blades *This also includes machete, throwing stars, knives longer than 4", and straight razors. Regular razors are permitted, and in my opinion, encouraged.*

Scissors with blades longer than 4 inches

Illegal drugs and substances, even if they're technically legal in your home state. *In some ports, sniffer dogs pass through the ship while passengers are off sunning themselves. Many cruisers who think a small amount of marijuana or a few pills would go unnoticed find themselves on a sudden flight home, mid cruise.*

Baseball bats

Hockey sticks

Cricket bats

Skateboards & surfboards

Bows & arrows

Aerial drones

Kites *(Did you know kites are encouraged on Washington state ferries? Not on cruise ships)*

Pets. *I know you'll miss your poochie-woochie, but pets are not allowed on ships. Of course, service animals are a different matter; just be sure to contact the cruise line well in advance. If the cruise line finds you've smuggled on your hamster, chicken, or cat, you and it will likely be let off the ship in the first available port. Don't chance it!*

Martial arts and/or self-defense gear, including handcuffs, pepper spray, night sticks.

Be aware of the ship's policy on buying weaponry, should you need any. In Alaska, it seemed everyone wanted ulu, super-sharp rocking kitchen knives. Reboarding the ship, the knives were confiscated and neatly tagged. On the last night, they were delivered to their owner's cabins, functionally arming the whole ship, scimitars, swords, ulu and all. On other cruise lines, hazardous items are simply not allowed onboard, flat out.

Travel Insurance

The whole topic of travel insurance is one that most people try to avoid as much as possible. For cruise travelers, about the only part that is more boring is the passenger contract. "It's better to have and not want, than to want and not have." That's my mother's wisdom there, applicable all over the place.

Whoever said "All publicity is good publicity" never ran a cruise line. Since so much of cruise business is generated through word of mouth, cruise lines can't afford bad press, and they go to great lengths to avoid something dire happening. Our cruise to the Mediterranean a couple of years ago had a port in southern Turkey cancelled "due to civil unrest" eight months before sailing. Fortune tellers, I guess; that city was really bad around the time we sailed.

Generally, if an area is known for extreme crime or pirates, etc, the cruise will simply detour to another port. They can't afford to put passengers at risk. In all but a very very small percentage of cruises, passengers have an uneventful vacation.

My criteria is "Can I afford to lose the money this cruise cost me?" and "Can I afford to fly home in a medical emergency?" For short, inexpensive cruises, I don't buy travel insurance. The opposite is also true.

Travel insurance is handy if you have a medical emergency at sea. The man who was attacked by his own appendix in the Straits of Messina ended up with a $123,000 bill, not including the hospital. Airlifting by one of those dangly helicopter baskets is not cheap. Let alone the fear factor.

Most policies allow 100% cancellation if a terrorist event occurs within thirty days of a cruise in any of the cities on the itinerary. I know this because I researched it before a recent cruise to a few places that had been on the evening news days before sailaway. We're fine; the cruise was uneventful, as by far the majority of them are.

In case of an unplanned adventure, be sure to get receipts, the names of those providing assistance and keep a journal of your experience. If nothing else, you'll have a great story, with details. Travel insurance is almost always secondary coverage. That's also good to know when considering the travel protection already provided by most credit cards, probably including the one you booked your cruise with. Look into what's already covered. My frugal soul balks at paying extra for what I already have.

Sometimes buying travel insurance is a foolish decision. That $29 one-night cruise an hour from home comes to mind. But sometimes it'd be foolish *not* to buy it. People who deal with chronic illness, or whose health is otherwise sensitive, would do well to think this one through. I wondered about the ninety-six year old woman who died on the ship an hour before we reached Gibraltar. Besides grieving her loss, and mentally beating themselves up for not accompanying her on a trans-Atlantic cruise, did her family have to pay a lot to get her home?

You can also buy insurance to protect you in case of any other type of catastrophe, including cancellation, a missed connection, lost or delayed baggage, or a dental or legal problem.

Don't feel stuck buying the insurance your cruise is selling. As in most things, you have a choice. Do a little research before checking the little box during the booking process. In a Situation, you might be surprised (and dismayed) at how little those cruise line policies cover. Trip-cancellation coverage benefits may not be paid out financially, and after a bad experience, you may not *want* a discount on another cruise. Medical coverage may be too limited. Personally, I want all the help I can get in a crisis. Coverage may also be limited to the cruise itself, not including sudden airfare or hotel stays. I prefer buying insurance through third-party companies, but it's up to you.

Cruise lines can't afford bad publicity. After getting roasted in the media over a ship-wide problem, they'll usually over pay above and beyond, regardless of who had insurance or not. You have to decide if you're more likely to experience a single-cabin event, or a full scale, on-the –evening- news cruise problem. No; both are highly unlikely!

As with most dilemmas in my life, I believe what's needed is more information. Feel free to read up, ask questions, use the toll-free 800 number that every insurance company offers. "What If?" is a fine start. If you have a medical condition that could cause a last-minute cancellation, you need to hear that it is covered. Plan for unknowns, too ... wait, you can't do that, by definition, unknowns are ... unknown. Oh, well; think about it! If Aunt Becky's medical condition worsens, or the grandson is born too early, or your elderly father goes to The Great Beach In The Sky the week before you sail, could you get your money back?

If something dreadful happens on the way to the cruise, during it, or on the way home, would you be covered for that, too? Does the policy cover things like sleeping on a park bench if your hotel reservation is cancelled, right at the check-in desk? Or missing a connecting flight in Germany?

Consider all resources. For example, If you graduated from a US university, check out AlumniAbroad.com. They offer alumni access to their comprehensive Travel Insurance Select policy which may be less expensive than some other policies, depending upon your age and total cost of your trip. Along these same lines, check out STATravel.com. They offer insurance to student travelers. Rates are based entirely on the length of your trip.

Which policy is right for you, if you opt for any? Most insurance companies offer a premium policy with all the bells and whistles, and a less expensive alternative with a little less coverage. Buy the policy that fits your needs. You're going to be the most well-read passenger on your cruise. Go practice now.

A final note: Buy the policy within the first couple of weeks or so from when you make your first cruise payment. That way, all pre-existing conditions will be covered. It'll save you from every having to prove a pre-existing conditioned *didn't* pre-exist. It's a pretty silly phrase. How on earth can anything *pre*-exist?

Embarkation Day: What to Expect

At last–enough calendar pages have flipped, and the cruise is finally here! You've done the planning, the packing, the flying-to-port. The ship looms in front of you, shining and bigger than you envisioned. Let's walk through what to expect as you board the ship. Bear in mind, if you've booked an extra exclusive stateroom, or are otherwise VIP status, there'll be slight variations, including escorts once you've checked in.

Unless you live across the street from the port, you'll arrive by vehicle, probably a car, a cab, a bus. In Vancouver, I saw a family arrive by horse-drawn carriage. Vehicles are channeled to various curbs, where excited people pour out, along with a few ho-hum, been-there-done-that types. Ignore them.

If you drove to the terminal, send the driver to park the car while the rest of you get out of the crowd and settle in for some fine people-watching. Yes, you can board while they park, but why would you? Much more fun to get on the ship together! Plus, you'll get the first impression of your fellow travelers. From sequined pantsuits to flannel jammies, I've seen it all. One woman sported a wide straw hat dripping with silk flowers and – I kid you not – six-inch dragonflies circling her head, on bouncy wires. Oh, yeah, you bet she made it into my last novel!

Porters will be right there to wrangle your suitcases. Unload your luggage, being mindful of the thousand or so other passengers who'd really like you to move it *along*, please, so they can board, too.

In your careful packing, you will have assured your passport, credit cards, and boarding documents are in your carry on. Double check; you can't get on the ship without them. Wailing, "But ... but ...they're in my *luggage!*" will not save you; trust me.

You should have dealt with your luggage tags already, the ones that tell the ship's crew which suitcases go to which cabin. If they came off, or you forgot, step aside. Let other people unload while you write out fresh tags. Porters carry a supply of blank luggage tags – just ask–but I advise writing it yourself. Embarkation Day is barely controlled, high-speed choreography, and you can't rely on a frenzied porter to write neatly. Don't bother listing your life's history on the tag; a surname and cabin number is fine. You *did* memorize your cabin number, right?

Hang onto to your carry on bag and your child's hand, and let the porter take your luggage. Slip the porter a couple of dollars for each bag. We'll generally tip around $5 for 2-3 bags, more if they're heavy. Not saying your luggage won't get on the ship if you fail to tip, but don't chance it.

Is your group together? Good! Follow the signs into the terminal. Security/Customs is next. Much like airport security, only friendlier, your carry ons will be scanned, and you'll likely pass through a metal detector. Get used to it; you'll repeat the process in every port. Some ports take it extremely seriously, other are more lax. In Europe, Husband's shoes set off every metal detector in every port. I suspect they had steel shanks. In most ports, the agents rescanned his shoes. In Turkey, the security guy merely shrugged him past, never leaving his chair.

Besides checking for risky items, the scanner also looks for contraband liquors and spirits. Again, this varies. In Spain, our travel mates bought a bottle of wine, expecting it would be confiscated until the last night. With no scanner onto the ship, they turned around, went back to the Duty Free shop in the terminal, and bought six more bottles. No, I'm not suggesting you try it.

Once Security/Customs is in your rearview mirror, head toward the check in area. Cruise lines hire land-based people to direct incoming passengers. That'd be a nice job; stand in a terminal a few hours a week, wishing excited people a happy trip, wouldn't it? Just follow directions, reading signs along the way. There may be more than one ship in port, so pay attention.

Depending on the port, and time of day, you may sit in a holding space until called, or go right to the check in agent. This part is easy, not much different than checking into a hotel. When it's your party's turn, hand over your passports and cruise documents. You'll be asked for a credit card to set up an onboard account. This is easiest, but you can also make arrangements in cash if you'd rather.

Somewhere in the process, you'll be required to fill out a very brief health evaluation form. It consists of your name, cabin number, and about five questions. Please be honest! Within reason, of course; if you know your stomach is angry because you ate six plates of fried jalapeno shrimp last night, you're not contagious. And, frankly, you deserve no sympathy.

But if you know you have a raging fever and you're pretty sure it's the flu or the plague or that virus that landed your sister in hospital last week, admit it. It's not wise to risk getting sicker at sea, and it's just wrong to put others at risk. What did they do to you?

Back to the check in. If you checked the yeah-I'm-sick boxes on your health form, you'll be sent for a quick evaluation by the ship's doctor. If all's in order, the check in process is smooth and quick. Hand over your boarding documents and credit card to the desk agent.

Soon you'll be handed your very own exclusive little plastic card. They go by different names on different cruise lines, but all serve the same purposes. In a cashless setting (the ship!), you'll use the card to purchase items onboard, like frou frou drinks and your seventh new watch. It's also your cabin door key. You must scan the card every time you leave or board the ship: a headcount, as well as your ID.

The key-card, by any other name, needs to be on your person the whole cruise, or at least within arm's reach. I reply on my ever-present pockets. Some fully grown adults opt for lanyards, the same ones you wore at summer camp when you were six. It's up to you. Just try not to lose the card, and be sure to keep it away from magnets and cell phones. Yes, you can get a replacement if you lose it or kill it, but try not to.

The card has your photo embedded in it, invisibly. That photo will either be taken at check in or when you set foot on the ship. Wanna guess which has the bigger grin?

On to the ship! Or maybe not; if the ship isn't boarding yet, you may need to wait a bit. You've probably been rushing all morning. Take time now to enjoy the moment. Your vacation is just a few feet away! Being where you are is a critical skill.

As you make your way to the gangway, you'll likely be greeted by the first of many photo ops. The ship's photographer has a backdrop, or a green screen, and will urge you to pose. Go ahead, if you wish; getting it taken costs nothing, although purchasing it later will. I usually say "No, thanks," because after traveling to the port and hauling my carry on, I'm not as cute as usual. Catch me when I've had a chance to comb my hair, please.

Past the photographers, on to the gangway, closer and closer to the ship! Scan your key-card into the slot as directed, and listen for the distinctive 'booonnngg' that officially signals the start of your cruise. That would make a fun ring tone for your phone. I've never seen it offered, but the Cruise Addict's phone has a ship's horn ring tone.

Some cruise lines go all out, welcoming passengers aboard with live music and champagne and white-dressed waiters passing out finger food and smiles. Others say, "Welcome" and that's it. On your way down the promenade deck, you'll see tables set up. Stop at the one for the kid's club, if you have young travelers with you. Sign them up, get their security bracelet if this cruise line uses them, pick up the schedule, and off you go. Other tables offer dining options in the specialty restaurants and beverage packages, as well as spa treatments. Stop, or walk by.

The cabins are likely to be ready mid-afternoon. Until then, all public areas are open, so go explore, find lunch, breathe, people watch ... The cruise is now yours!

Make time to walk everywhere on the ship sometime during the cruise, if not the first day. Ships have beautiful artwork and sculptures and colors in the most unusual places. There's usually unique artwork in each stairwell, which you can use as landmarks; your cabin's on the deck with the wild horses running through surf.

Pools and hot tubs are open on the first day – as are waterslides– and they're usually not crowded simply because many cruisers don't think to use them. If you're interested, don't forget to pack a bathing suit in your carry-on bag. Smile at the envious glances of the people still wearing heavy sweatshirts. They're from Michigan, and leaving home in a blizzard can make a person forget swimming is available in a Florida port that very same day.

First Day Onboard

Let's approach this in terms of Dos and Don'ts. No, let's skip the Don'ts; you have enough negativity in your life, right?

First, do read up on cruise line policies, including boarding times. On embarkation day, passengers must be onboard at least two hours ahead of the sailing time. In subsequent ports, it's usually thirty minutes before sailing. Double check your printed daily planner and the signboard by the gangway to be sure. And don't cut it too close. I could tell you stories.

You can usually board as soon as the previous passengers sadly admit their vacation is over and drag themselves off the ship. The last to disembark can be as late as eleven o'clock. Generally, passengers begin boarding within half an hour or so after that, soon as ship is swept for stowaways and the security systems reset. Early-arriving VIPs, and fancy suite passengers board first, then everyone else, as they arrive. If you arrive around 11:30 for a later-afternoon sailing, you'll get on fairly quickly, unless the other 2000 passengers had same idea.

Have a little patience. You're only in charge of yourself, as I keep telling the kids, not other people. If several hundred passengers arrive at the port around the same time, you may have to wait in a significant line or two. Make like a Boy Scout and be prepared. Having a granola bar to stave off whining from hungry children (or spouse) can make things more pleasant for all concerned.

I packed new sock puppets in the carry on when we traveled with small grandchildren. The new-toy novelty helped pass the time in line, and puppets are silent. That new (and loud) video game you downloaded for the hand held device may not be appreciated by people around you. Would I rather hear a whining child or a shrieking video game? Really, are those my only choices?

Some passengers wait until last minute to make a run for the check in line; on our first cruise only four boarded after our group. In my defense, and I guess I need one, we were driving to port with friends, who were running late, and then we were lost detouring around some construction. Maybe not lost, just temporarily misplaced. For the record, I firmly believe those handy little Detour signs with arrows are to be trusted.

Do take photos −lots of them. Get that first "Hooray, I'm on vacation" shot of your family by the ship's rail; snap a pic of your cabin in pristine condition before it's cluttered with daily schedules, towel animals, and your assorted belongings. Capture interesting spots onboard before they're overrun with passengers. This may be your only chance to get pictures of the empty pool, barren atrium, etc, unless you're like Husband, who is a night-wanderer. He loves having the ship to himself in the middle of the night. So long as he doesn't slam the cabin door, I can ignore him.

Do explore the ship, and check out places you're especially interested in. A free facial? This is the time to volunteer to be a model for the spa tour later on, if you don't mind a parade of strangers staring at your seaweed-covered face. Locate the specialty restaurants that most interest you. Sometimes, they offer samples. Go ahead and make reservations now, if you know when you'd like to dine there; asking about 'first day' price breaks.

On the other hand, do be flexible, unafraid to play it by ear. While large groups often need reservations, if there are just two or three of you, you can often get into reserved shows and specialty dining at the last minute. Cruise lines always hold back some openings onboard.

One exception: if you're heartset on a particular and popular tour, you'd better jump on it, because spaces fill up fast on popular shore excursions. However, I still think you're better off booking a private tour in port, on your own, ahead of time. You may not know if you'll be in the mood for a steakhouse or Asian dinner months from now, but you know you'll want to tour Pompeii while you're in port.

Do explore the ship. Do I sound repetitive? While your cabin probably won't be available for a while, all public areas are open on embarkation day. If you're as vigilant as we are, then you have probably read tons of reader reviews, studied the deck plans, looked up ship photos online, and know everything about the ship and your itinerary. Still, there is much you can discover once you step foot on the ship. You're really on the ship! Go look around!

You'll likely get a ship's deck plan as you board. If not, make the Guest Services desk a close-to-first stop. I suggest that you start at the top deck of the ship and work your way down, so you end your tour in the lobby area, where reception is located. Staff members can answer any questions you have after your exploration. Plus, down is easier than up; thirteen flights of stairs is a bit much. Be sure to greet any passing crew. Your mama taught you manners, yes?

Do find lunch. You may as well eat; you paid for it!
On embarkation day, crew and staff will often herd
passengers to the buffet, but other venues are often open.
Cafes, a dining room, snack bars, poolside grill; read your
daily schedule, the one they handed you upon boarding. You
might find it on your bed, and there's always one posted near
the Guest Services desk. Or just ask a crewmember where to
find an alternative for a calmer first meal. Crew members are
stationed all over the ship to help passengers find their way.
And don't gobble everything in sight. Dinner's just a few
hours away, and you have all cruise long to sample the foods
offered.

Do plan on waiting to head to your cabin. The staff is
busy cleaning and preparing the room for you; the public
areas are done first. Listen for announcements on when the
staterooms' corridors will open.

Cabins are not generally ready until 12:30-1 p.m. The
public areas are all open as soon as passengers board. You can
grab a snack, take pictures, ooh and ahh as needed. Be aware
you'll have to haul your carry ons bags with you until your
cabin is ready. On some ships, there's a designated area where
you can check your carry ons, but we never use it. It's just one
more line to stand in on a day I'd rather explore. Make that
two more lines: dropping off as well as retrieving later.

Once the staterooms are open, Do meet your
stateroom attendant. A cabin steward can enhance your
vacation in ways you haven't thought of. They're having a
crazy busy day, but will stop by to greet you as soon as they
can find a minute to spare. This is your chance to get to
acquainted, briefly, and make any special requests, such as
reconfiguring the beds, a flatter or fatter pillow, extra pillow

or hangers, ice twice daily, and so on. Be polite and appreciative; they have the power to add to your cruise greatly in little ways, or just do the basics.

Do get the first-day chores out of the way as soon as you can, so you can quit thinking about it. We tag-team wiping every cabin surface with a disinfectant wipe, which I packed from home in my carry on. Yes, I know the stateroom is clean, but no stray germ is going to spoil my trip if I can help it. We swipe the phone, remote control, door knobs, drawer pulls, light switches; anything human hands may have touched. I tried disinfectant spray once. Bad idea; ruined the shine of the metal surfaces, and I spent a good ten minutes re-buffing them!

Do unpack and organize your stuff. Luggage will be placed outside your door as soon as they get to it. I've seen those workers—they're literally running to finish! So be patient. When your bags arrive, haul them inside and unpack. I know you don't want to, but it'll make the rest of the cruise easier, so do it anyway. Again, we have the tag-teaming down to a science; I hand stuff to Husband and he puts it away, hanging shirts up, dividing the closet and shelf space evenly, while I unpack and arrange the desk area.

Do resolve now to keep the cabin as tidy as possible! Besides the embarrassment factor – you don't want your steward to think you're a slob, do you? – you'll be more relaxed in an orderly cabin. Not too extreme, mind you. I visited our friend's cabin on Day Four and at first glance, I thought they hadn't brought anything with them. The cabin looked as barren as ours did before we arrived! That neatnik gene missed me.

Do continue your goal of being the most–informed person on the ship, minus the staff and crew. They were here first. Read the daily schedule the check in agent handed you (or it might be in your cabin). See what's going on, which venues are open for lunch, what the first night's show will be, when is the drawing for free spa treatments, etc. If you never read, you'll never know.

I've met passengers on ships who astounded me with their ignorance. I don't mean dim-wittedness; they can't help that. But to stand there on Day Four, not knowing there's an adult-only pool, a skating rink, daily high tea at four-thirty, a theater, just appalls me. You may never use the putt putt golf course, but at least acknowledge its existence.

I even met a man disembarking on Day Nine who said he was greatly disappointed with the entertainment. He'd been led to believe the ship had wonderful shows, but all he saw was the piano bar singer, night after night. He about wore a path in the floor, walking from his cabin to the buffet to the piano bar, and back, and nowhere else on board. You may choose to participate or not, but know your options.

Do watch for a bargain, especially if it's on something you wanted already. Embarkation day discounts abound. Most folks are checking out the ship and getting settled in on the first day, not paying attention. Check out the "embarkation day specials" when you board. Spas most always have a buy-something-get-something special.

Also, specialty restaurants people haven't happened upon yet are easy to get reservations at on the first night. Plus, they usually offer a bonus, maybe a free bottle of wine or a discount if you dine on embarkation day. Look for internet and spa discounts, too. Tour the spa early, and they might invite you to be a model for one of their treatments later on. Not me; I think I lost a few layers of skin during a dermabrasion demo.

I admit I'm not good at this myself, but Do try to pace yourself. Most likely, you've had a long flight or a drive to the port, and that's tiring before you step foot on the ship! But the excitement of the first day is undeniable. Even after all our cruises, I still get bubbles of excitement under my ribs when I step on a ship. Bring it on! I want to do it all, see it all! Really, you have the entire vacation to do and see everything. You don't have to do it all in the first hour.

Do make your last phone calls, texts and tweets while your phone can access land-based cell towers and you're not paying sky-high satellite Internet and roaming fees. Post that cheesy *we're-on-vacation!* photo for your friends to envy, then park your phone in the safe. You're on vacation ... *vacate*, already!

Check Your Stateroom

Although you can board early, the steward can't let you into your stateroom until every one of the cabins is ready, no matter how wonderful you are, so save your breath. As soon as you can, locate your room and check it thoroughly. I check mine while I'm wiping it with the disinfectant wipe; two birds, one stone. If there are any defects or issues, report them right away. Your steward probably never sat in your desk chair, and can't know the thing sags like Aunt Kate's famous birthday cakes unless you mention it. Burned out lightbulbs, too, might escape the steward's notice.

If you find a serious cabin issue, like a broken window or mold in the bathroom, bring it to the crew's attention immediately. Most cruises are sold out, and you stand a greater chance of moving to a better cabin by being among the first to request a change.

Sit on the bed. If it's too hard –many are—now's the time to request help. Some ships keep a stash of foam egg crate mattress toppers, but they're limited. First complain, first get. On a recent 15-day trans-Atlantic cruise, I found the bed not quite as soft as my dining room table at home. Between my arm falling asleep, then my hip throbbing, then my back screaming, then my other shoulder aching, then my neck cramping, different body parts taking turns wailing ... it was not a restful night! And did I tell you there were fourteen more nights to follow?

I mentioned it to my cabin steward the first morning. Actually, she asked why I was limping. She was too polite to bring up the dark bags under my eyes, the size of my carry-on. The steward sadly told me the cruise line had recently done away with the cushy mattress pads in favor of all new mattresses. At turn down that night, she added four layered sheets, which helped a little. Now the bed was as soft as my dining room table with a tablecloth on it.

Tossing and turning all night, I had nightmares when I did fall asleep, including a very vivid dream about being in labor, birthing an elephant. My subconscious obviously felt sorry for me. Every morning, I woke up aching; every day our steward asked how I'd slept. Her concern grew, along with the dark circles under my eyes. With nine straight sea days, I couldn't exactly run out and buy a mattress pad in port.

Sleep deprivation is a common torture tactic, you know. I took to napping on deck in the afternoons. Each night, I debated about sleeping on the floor, or in the desk chair, either of which was softer than the bed. By Day Four, I hadn't slept more than two consecutive hours, I was living on Tylenol, and wishing I'd never left home.

On Day Six, the Hotel Director's assistant did a spot check. "Is the cabin satisfactory? Is the steward doing her job?"

Cabin's fine, love the steward, but that *bed!* Stricken, the man sputtered about how the cruise line had spent millions on brand new mattresses, they'd heard very few complaints, etc.

"Sit down," I ordered.

He plopped on the bed, and promptly stood up, rubbing his backside. "I will see to it myself," he promised.

Returning to the cabin that evening, we laughed. The bed looked a lot like the one in the Princess and the Pea story, half a foot taller and undeniably plump. What on earth ...? Someone had laid twelve bed pillows under the bottom sheet, end to end, and side to side in a checkerboard pattern, literally a *pillow* top mattress! It may have been intended as a joke. I didn't care; for the rest of the cruise, I slept like I was on a cloud.

You may ask, why didn't I complain louder? After all I've written a whole book on complaining. I knew before we boarded (because I read current reviews of the ship) the ship that RCCL had recently replaced all of the mattresses, and done away with the germy-but-soft egg-crate mattress toppers. You gotta know when complaining has a chance of being effective.

Muster Drill

Yes, of course you can decide how to spend time on your vacation ... just not during the muster drill. It's non-negotiably mandatory, even if you have cruised before, even if you can recite the canned announcements in your sleep. You have to go. And be on time; it doesn't start until the stragglers mosey in, and that's time wasted for everyone. Not sure what to expect? Here you go.

The International Maritime Organization (IMO) requires that all passenger cruise ships hold a safety drill within 24 hours of embarkation. These emergency drills typically occur before departure; time can vary. We've been on several cruises that held the drill on Day Two. Since the Costa Concordia ran aground before their muster drill, ships are more strict about holding them early. On quite a few cruises, passengers do a muster drill just before sailaway, then head on up to the party.

Passengers are notified prior to the drill (repeatedly!) and all venues are closed for the duration of the practice. You'll be told whether or not to bring life vests from the staterooms. Listen, because you don't want to be the only one hauling bulky orange vests around the ship if you don't have to. Most cruise lines have done away with this requirement. Seems people were getting injured at the safety drill, tripping one another, which kinda defeats the purpose. These trailing straps can be a hazard.

Passengers are guided to specified meeting points, either in an inside lounge or theater or on an outer deck under the lifeboats. During the drill, crewmembers will give instructions on what to do in case of an emergency and demonstrate how to put on life jackets. The idea is for you to locate your assigned muster station, and get an idea what to do in case of an emergency. The instructions cover how to put on a life vest, and talks about hazards at sea. Did you know fire is the biggest risk?

Chances you will ever need to know this information are low, but pay attention anyway. Often passengers take it lightly, talking and griping during the drill, but it really is there for your protection. If you can't be still for a 10 minute safety presentation, how could you handle a real life problem? In a real emergency, you'd want to the information to be fresh in your mind, and what doesn't go in, isn't there to remember later on.

Every crew member–even the entertainers—has a dual assignment on the ship, one of which is to know what to do in an emergency. These include manning muster stations, directing passengers, evacuating the kids' club, assisting disabled passengers, and so on.

During the muster drill, the ship's horn will sound the standard warning: seven short horn blasts followed by one long one. If you have young children with you, take a minute to alert them, "It's about to get noisy," and cover their sensitive ears. I've heard more than one scared child go off like a siren, nearly drowning out the ship's horn, because she had not been forewarned.

Failure to comply has resulted in passengers being forced to disembark the ship, yes, on Day One. Just ask the fellow removed from Holland America's *Westerdam* at the pier in Fort Lauderdale, Florida, or the elderly couple kicked off Seabourn's luxurious *Seabourn Sojourn* in Lisbon, Portugal, for refusing to attend the drill. Both incidents occurred after the fatal *Costa Concordia* disaster in 2012, when they should have known better.

Note that a lot of standing is often involved during the muster drill. Notify a crewmember if this is a problem. There's a lounge set aside for those with special needs. If you have mobility issues or small children, be sure to notify your cabin steward and Guest Services the very first day. A cabin steward will provide you with child-size life vests. In a crisis, you don't want your little one squirting through the neck opening.

Health & Avoiding Illness

I know you spent a lot of money, weeks reading up on the ship, and ports, and underlining my books, but if you come down ill, please have the good sense to cancel the cruise. If you're coughing up your left lung, or having a kidney stone flare up, you'll be miserable on the trip. Plus, you might be contagious, and it's inconsiderate to put other vacationers at risk.

Of course, things occur with no warning. I've been on at least three cruises where a person had to be airlifted off the ship in the throes of acute appendicitis, which they didn't have the previous week. Unforeseen accidents, heart attacks, strokes, kidney stones, etc, can all occur out of the blue, but if you have an inkling Things Are Gonna Be Bad, just book a different cruise later on. It's not worth the risk. Imagine being sick at sea, with limited medical resources.

On the other hand, don't walk in fear. If you're in reasonable health, with nothing dire on the horizon, go for it! Some of our favorite fellow passengers were well into their nineties, full of energy and good humor. And they were killer on the trivia questions.

You're no more or less likely to be attacked by your appendix or gall bladder at sea than anywhere else. Some things are random. Other ailments are somewhat predictable. Those, you should prepare for. Of course, bring along any prescription medicines you routinely take, along with a basic first aid kit. I keep mine in a sandwich size zip-type bag. It's just a trip; I don't need the 460 mega pack of bandages. Just a few will do nicely. Toss in a small supply of basic medicines.

Think antacid, aspirin, anti-diarrhea pills, pain remedies, anti-itch crème, that sort of thing. They're expensive to purchase onboard, if they're even in stock.

I'm sure you hardly give your teeth a second thought, but if you get a toothache, it'll shoot up your priority list. An emergency dental care kit is a good thing to pack. Also, be gentle flossing on a cruise, or any other extended vacation. Those expensive bridges and crowns can be pulled loose if you floss aggressively. If you're going to do that, it's certainly better to do it within shouting distance of your favorite dentist.

Even if you're lazy about it at home, wear sunscreen on a cruise. If you sail mid-winter, it's easy to let sunscreen slip your mind. We took a Caribbean cruise in February. The ship had a strong contingent from New York City, including several hundred police and fire department members. Winter was severe at home, and you've never seen such a sad bunch of blistered people by Day Three!

You can just as easily get burned walking the streets of Europe in the summer, kayaking or scenic cruising in Alaska and doing just about anything in the strong sun of Australia as you can by sun-bathing poolside. While it can be a pain to apply and re-apply your SPF 30, you will be in greater pain if you burn. Plus, sun damage can rear its ugly head decades later. Ask any dermatologist; most of their skin cancer patients are elderly, and each has a story about a bad sunburn when they were a child.

If you get sick on a cruise ship, it's likely you were infected by a co-worker or that grimy grocery cart at home.

Nevertheless, here are some common sense tips to stay healthy:

Start out healthy. If you're in the middle of chemotherapy with no measurable immune system, going anywhere with a couple of thousand folks and their own germs isn't a great idea.

Running yourself ragged finishing those last few things before the cruise can make you more susceptible to illness. Exhibit A: our friend Brian, working frantically before a flight to Iceland, frantically tapping on his laptop at the airport departure gate, cell phone at his ear, finishing the things he didn't have time to do because he'd been up the previous twenty hours rewiring his house. Even if you can avoid jet lag, starting a trip when you're just a little beat up feels awful. If you possibly can, get to the departure city at least a day early to catch your breath.

Drink more water than usual. Between the sea air, food that has more salt than you probably use at home, a pre-cruise flight or two, and some glorious tropical beaches, dehydration can be a real issue. Inside your nostrils, there are tiny hairs; everybody's, not just yours. Their job is to capture the majority of viruses and bacteria that try to invade your system. Did you even know those tiny knights are there, barring the door, in effect? They don't use teensy swords, but they do pass out on the battlefield if they get dried out. Drink, to fortify the troops.   Drinking water also cuts down on headaches, and helps your digestive system do its job. Sipping water is the first defense against seasickness, too.

If you're especially prone to dehydration in hot weather, or one of those athletic types who sees nothing wrong with eleven basketball games on the top deck in the Caribbean sunshine, you're better off guzzling a sports drink with electrolytes. If you're that kind of person, you know the brand. You can buy single-serving drink mixes at home to put in your ever-present water bottle.

Water with meals is good, although perhaps not as much as Husband consumes. Not that I'd call him a sponge, mind you, but I cannot figure out how a man can drink that much water without a bucket at his feet. It's almost comical! The waiters try to keep his water glass full, over and over again, during a meal. Usually they will comment. A few times, they've silently given up and brought Husband *two* water glasses. Dehydration is not an issue for him. Can a person drown from drinking too much water?

I know I just told you to drink a lot of water, but in some destinations (Mexico, Africa, and Egypt come to mind), it's not necessarily safe to drink local water. In risky areas, you'll want to drink only beverages in sealed bottles to avoid getting sick, and avoid ice. North Americans tend to prefer cold drinks, unlike the rest of the planet. In Turkey, I noticed that every person who bought a bottle of water was 'profiled." Americans were handed cold bottles from the cooler, while others were given bottles from that pallet over there, without fail. If you have a choice of risking your health by adding ice to your drink ... don't do it.

Only eat fruits you peeled yourself, and don't think washing vegetables in tainted water cleans them. Be alert to anything that goes near your mouth, and I mean *anything*.

I remember that week in Mexico, where I spent a couple of days perched in the bathroom, clutching a waste basket, wondering if dying or recovering was more likely. My father was the only one in our group not felled by Montezuma's Revenge, alias "La Tourista" virus. I'd been fanatical about drinking only bottled beverages, and using baby wipes on my hands ... how'd I get that sick?

Finally, it came to me: my toothbrush. I turned on my Dad, demanding to know how he dared stay healthy when the rest of us were in God's own waiting room. Didn't he brush his teeth?

Shrugging, he waved at the tequila bottle. "Don't drink the water."

It takes a hardy tourist to rinse his toothbrush in tequila.

Norovirus and Zika

Does it seem to you they're inventing new and different problems? Norovirus isn't new, and it's not limited to cruise ships, either. Breakouts occur in day camps, college campuses, nursing homes, conventions, and that family reunion some years ago, the one I try to block out of my memory. You hear about it more on cruise ships simply because cruise lines are required to report even minor outbreaks, and other places are not.

If you're not already fanatical about hand washing, develop that habit ASAP. Cruise ships have gel hand sanitizer available –some more than others–but all are anti-bacterial. Norovirus, common cold, and the flu are all *viruses*, untouchable by anti-bacterial stuff.

The number one way to avoid getting sick with Norovirus or other illnesses on a cruise is to thoroughly wash your hands, more than you ordinarily would; before and after you eat, after you use the restroom, when returning to the cruise ship after a day in port and every time you touch a stranger or an oft-touched item like a stairway railing, a salad scoop in the buffet, or a slot machine. It's all in your hands, so to speak.

Do an online search for how to avoid Norovirus, and you'll learn enough to make you skip dinner. The main things you need to know are: it's a very common, highly contagious virus, spreads easily, and it can knock victims so flat they can't even try to hide the symptoms. It hits about 20,000 people every year. All but an itsy bitsy number recover fully

within a week, left only with a foul memory. The vicious
virus attacks the stomach and intestines with a vengeance.

It can be mistaken for "stomach flu" although it's not
flu at all, or "food poisoning," but it's not related to food. It's
quite possible you've already had Noro in your life, and you
lived to tell. If you're looking for a way to get out of your
scheduled cruise, don't let this be it.

Norovirus is typically spread through physical contact
with ill people or surfaces/objects they may have touched. On
many cruise ships, captains ban shaking hands, insisting on
fist-bump greetings. Really, both are silly, when you think
about it. Going up to a new person, grasping a body part and
pumping it up and down is not much different than making a
fist and thumping a new friend.

For the most part, Norovirus outbreaks are the results
of guests setting sail already sick, and passing it around. Once
a person has been exposed to Norovirus, it takes anywhere
from one to three days for its symptoms to appear. Symptoms
typically last only 24 to 48 hours, but people may be
contagious for as long as two weeks after recovery. Keep up
the handwashing!

If you come down with the dreaded gastrointestinal
symptoms, call the ship's medical center. Noro is a touchy
subject; they'll probably make a cabin-call, rather than asking
you to go to the Medical center. All they can do is tell you to
avoid dehydration, and stay in your cabin. Believe me, if you
get Norovirus, you won't feel up to being more than four feet
from your bathroom anyway.

If more than one percent of passengers exhibit Norovirus symptoms, the ship goes into Red status. Crewmembers clean even more thoroughly than usual, with stronger solvents, including bleach on handrails and elevator buttons. Buffet service often switches from "help yourself" to manned stations. Salt and pepper shakers may disappear from tables, and warnings about handwashing will be stepped up. It'll run its course, pardon the pun, in a couple of days, then all will return to normal.

Zika is a new and scary-sounding issue. No, it's not new; it's been in Africa for a long time, named after the Zika Valley. We westerners are just now getting around to paying attention to it. Due to our if-it's-not-bothering-*me*-it's-not-important attitude, we're behind the eight ball, now that it's spreading to our neck of the woods. Researchers scramble to figure out what all it affects and how to fight the problem, years too late.

Here's the quick run-down: Zika is real, and worth paying attention to. It's transmitted by a specific mosquito that lives in tropical and sub tropical parts of the world, including the Caribbean and lower US states. While many mosquitoes tend to bite at dusk and dawn, these mean little critters are aggressive daytime biters, as well as at night. There is no vaccine or treatment for Zika.

The best way to avoid getting sick with Zika virus is to avoid getting bitten by infected mosquitos. You can do this by staying away from areas on the map where the little buggers live, but, if you're not pregnant, don't let a tiny insect ruin your plans. If you go to Zika-prone areas, protect yourself from mosquito bites by covering your body, and using DEET-based insect repellant liberally, both on your clothing and yourself.

80% of people bitten by a mosquito infected with Zika will display no symptoms. Those who do get sick usually have mild-to-ignorable symptoms, including bright red eyes for a few days, low grade fever, rash, joint pain. To date, only one person in America has died from Zika, an elderly person who already had multiple medical issues.

The biggest risk is to our unborn population, the most vulnerable segment of humanity. A pregnant woman who's infected can pass Zika on to her baby. The experts warn of horrific birth defects, but research into other neurologic issues arising later in life is ongoing. Because long-term problems are not known, it's best to take very precaution.

The US Center for Disease Control is the top expert, and their recommendation is clear: **"Pregnant women should not travel to areas with Zika."**

Read http://cdc.gov for the most up to date information.

Cruise lines are good about letting pregnant passengers cancel or change their cruises with no penalty; make the call if you're at extra risk.

Before our recent trip to Puerto Rico, a discussion broke out online about Zika. Some passengers brushed it aside. Two women who were considering pregnancy cancelled their cruise, wisely. Others planned to take reasonable precautions. Some others talked about odd-sounding remedies, including oil of orange in their ear canals and using a particular brand of laundry detergent to mask mosquito-attracting odor (which doesn't help, in case you were wondering).

A few people said, "No problem, I'm not going to get off the ship in Puerto Rico. The mosquitos won't come on the ship."

What?? Did they forget mosquitos *fly*? Even if they didn't fly, it's certainly easy for any insect to hitch a ride on a returning passenger in any port. The ship has no force field over it, no protective dome to keep mosquitos at bay. No, people who go to these areas are not safe anywhere from a beastie that requires only a bottle cap of water to raise its family. If you're going, take precautions –reasonable ones. Eating raw onions for breakfast is no defense against a virus.

As it turned out, on our recent cruise, no one was bitten, or showed Zika symptoms. A cruise ship can be a gossipy place; I think we'd have heard about it. Personally, mosquitos find me delicious. If there's a bug anywhere around, I'm usually the one they flock to. In Puerto Rico, I wore DEET spray, and didn't score a single munch-mark. I'd have noticed. Besides being tasty, I'm also allergic to mosquito bites, with bites often swelling to the size of a sliced golf ball.

Seasickness

A lovely cruise can quickly be spoiled if you're beset by waves of nausea from the up and down and side to side motion of a cruise ship. New ships are remarkably stable, so your chances of feeling green are not very high, but we'd better talk about what to do if you're one of the 'lucky' few.

First, quit beating yourself up. Although it does seem to run in families, seasickness is not a sign of weakness; it can strike anyone. On our last trans-Atlantic cruise, crew members who had spent the last five months in the calm Caribbean fell like flies after we passed Cuba. Fully 180 of them were lined up at the Medical Center for a shot of whatever that miraculous stuff is, officers included. And those people *live* on a cruise ship!

Plan ahead if you're especially prone to motion sickness. Rough waters can be anticipated by itinerary and the time of year you're sailing. Generally, in the winter months, seas are rougher, especially in the Atlantic. You might be happier with a nice, mild itinerary, not one that goes around Cape Horn, for example. Port-intensive cruises tend to be calmer than those on the wide ocean blue. River cruises, which move slower than walking pace, don't trigger seasickness.

Rough seas or not, remember that it won't last long. If you know you have a history of motion sickness, err on the side of booking a more stable cabin. Rocking motion is less likely to be felt midships, and on lower decks. Locations on the far ends of the ship do move more than the middle.

Need a visual? Hold a pencil by the middle, and wiggle it in your hand. See how both ends move more than the middle? If you get sick between your home and the corner grocer, that's the spot you'd better book your cabin. A deluxe suite at the front of the ship might come with all the bells and whistles, but you won't be able to enjoy them with your head in the toilet.

Passengers swear by the pretty Sea-Band acupressure wristbands. I've encountered too many folks with those patches behind their ears, complaining of dire symptoms, to recommend them, but you do as you see fit. Possible hallucinations, temporary blindness, heart issues, double vision ... not for me, thanks. If you think about it at home, bring some powdered ginger root capsules, sold in the vitamin/supplement aisle. One son tends to turn green at sea, and when he goes with us, somebody always packs these.

If you're feeling queasy, don't run out to the ship's doctor. There are a slew of remedies to try before you throw in that towel. Symptoms usually start with a headache. Guest Services Desk can give you packets of both pain pills and seasick medicine, for free, saving a trip to Medical.

Stay hydrated, and I mean with water; alcohol will only magnify your symptoms. As with morning sickness, having an empty stomach also makes things worse. Room service can bring you green apples and bland crackers (crew members swear by the apple remedy). Ginger is a tried-and-true remedy; again, available onboard. Ginger ale, ginger candies, gingersnaps and candied ginger all work; just be sure it's real, not "ginger flavored." Ask your waiter, cabin steward, or call room service.

A cabin steward told our daughter-in-law, who turned greenish during a 22-hour long storm, to bruise an orange and sniff the peel. She was in no mood to try it, but at least she didn't throw the orange at him. He brought her some meds from the Guest Services desk. Within an hour, she felt great, and hungry for a chili cheese dog. I'm not prone to motion sickness, but *that* made me queasy.

If nausea hits, override your natural instinct to go lie down in your cabin. Fresh air, and looking FAR, can help dramatically in the early stages of remembering your stomach isn't made of steel. Looking for distant whale spouts will ease your tummy, whereas doing small close work, like beadwork or reading, can make you feel worse. Going outdoors, cool breezes and looking at the distant horizon helps most people immediately. The horizon thing is why people who tend to be carsick demand the driver's or front passenger seat. A cool towel or even ice on your neck seems to help quickly.

Seasickness doesn't last long, but if symptoms get severe, call Medical onboard. They have medicines available that'll help you get back up and dancing pretty fast. It involves a needle in the behind: I warned you.

Security Onboard

All told, your chances of becoming a crime statistic are lower on a cruise vacation than almost any other vacation, short of camping in your own backyard. Even then, there's risk of that big tree falling on your tent. You may have heard that cruise ships are not safe, due to international/ maritime laws, which can make crime stats fall between the cracks, or the decking boards, in this case. If you're a rule-breaker, a pusher-of-common-boundaries, or a criminal, you're right; cruising can be a potential problem. If you're just an ordinary soul, and keep your wits about you, you'll be fine.

Just don't take needless chances. If you act smart, cruising is no more hazardous than touring any big city. Probably safer: What kind of a criminal would pay for a cruise when there are plenty of potential victims on the planet?

Every time you enter your cabin, check the bathroom and closet while the cabin door is still open. Use the same precautions that you would when entering a hotel room. Being cautious never hurt anyone. Don't leave valuables lying around in your cabin. Put your wallet and valuables in the cabin's safe or the purser's safe. Be sure to use all the locks on the door when you are asleep. Don't open the door to strangers. Protect your cabin key and cabin number. Use your God-given common sense; if you'd hesitate on land, don't do it at sea. Stay in the public areas, and remember that even though the other passengers are friendly, you don't really know them.

With a couple thousand passengers from varying backgrounds onboard, a ship is like a small city. Most folks are wonderful, happy to be on vacation. Others may have a propensity for evil, or lose their good judgment in the face of too much alcohol. Keep your wits about you!

If you are cruising with your children, set rules just as you do at home. Establish curfews for your teenagers, and caution them to not accompany crew members to non-public areas. Keep close eye on your children. I've seen nine- and eleven-year-olds running around a ship, playing in elevators, etc, unsupervised. Would you let you child run through downtown at home alone? Any of those doors could have a Bad Person behind them, and it takes just seconds to snatch up a child. They're only little.

General safety rules apply on cruise ships, same as anywhere else. Don't accept drinks from strangers, be aware of your surroundings, don't go into a stranger's room, and keep your cabin door locked at all times. There's a little peephole in most cabin doors, but our rule is, if we didn't invite anyone, we never open the door. Room service counts as an invitation.

As an adult, don't leave your good judgement at home, either. Sexual and other assaults do occur on ships. It's never a smart idea to get so intoxicated your reason is clouded, nor is it smart to go off with a stranger you just met. Being on a cruise ship doesn't negate the need for you to use common sense.

Using common sense is the best way to prevent falling overboard, too. Railings are a prescribed height, above an adult's center of gravity. Watching the dolphins won't cause you to go overboard. Playing tightrope walker on your balcony railing very well could. Instruct children to keep their feet firmly on the floor at all times. Never stand on a chair to see over the railing better. And for heaven's sake, never sit your baby on the railing, even if you have your hand on them! I've seen parents do that, and it made me feel like smacking them. If his judgement is that lacking, how will he ever raise that child to adulthood?

Minor injuries happen on ships, same as everywhere else. Falling down stairs, stubbing your toe, breaking a finger playing basketball, dancing ...little injuries are fairly common. You should bring a first aid kit onboard, but if it's anything Big, don't hesitate to track down the medical staff onboard. If it's the cruise line's fault, be sure to document the incident.

A few years ago, my mother was perusing the ship's book selection. The ship listed a bit, and the heavy glass bookcase door fell off, breaking her toe. Turns out Maintenance had neglected to replace the screws; the door was just set in place. Mom's medical bills were covered by the cruise line. After a polite letter detailing all she had missed on the cruise because of her injury, Mom received a free cruise certificate in the mail. The cruise line screwed up, and they knew it.

Passenger Behavior

When you sign on for a cruise, you agree in your cruise contract to a code of conduct, promising not to do anything inappropriate, discourteous, or blatantly unsafe. Break the rules, and shipboard security personnel may confine you to your cabin, or worse, send you to the brig.

There are quite a few ways to get in trouble on a cruise ship, same as anywhere else on the planet. Some infractions, while seeming funny through a drunken haze, can get you confined to the ship's brig, and kicked off in the nearest port. In that case, you're on your own getting home; even a pleading to story to your travel insurance company may not help. And don't even ask for a refund.

Teens can get into trouble onboard with alcohol consumption. Technically, ship's drinking age is 21, with the following proviso: *Passengers ages 18 to 20, with the written consent of their parents or guardian, can purchase beer or wine for themselves only when the ship is sailing in international waters (except in Alaska and Hawaii, where passengers must be 21 years of age to consume or purchase alcohol or any kind).*

In reality, it's not that hard for a kid to get the stuff. It's even easier in Mexican ports, where the legal drinking age is, "whoever has money." My simple rule when we cruised with our teens: "Don't do anything that would require me to talk to Security or identify your body," along with a reminder that I had the power to make their lives oh, so very miserable.

You can be booted for even a simple argument in the casino, or punching out that obnoxious guy at the bar. A few years ago, an elderly couple leaped into trouble on *Cunard's Queen Mary 2* after the wife started a shouting match with a fellow passenger. According to an official statement from the cruise line, the 82-year-old woman "engaged in multiple incidences of disrespectful and disruptive behavior toward crew members and other guests." And the 91-year-old husband joined in, ultimately punching an officer. Only a few days into a thirty-day, $20,000 cruise, both husband and wife were confined to their cabin until they were removed at the next port. I can't think of a disagreement worth yelling over, at that cost.

Although drug laws are morphing in parts of America, traditionally illegal drugs are still illegal on cruise ships. You may think, "Heck, this is my vacation, and I can do what I want." You do, but not when it comes to breaking the law — even if the stuff is legal at home.

Under the Cruise Vessel Security and Safety Act, crew members are required to report seeing or smelling anything suspicious. Get caught with even one joint, and you'll be kicked off the ship at the next port, and probably turned over to local authorities. A Mexican jail makes anyone think twice!

In many ports, police dogs may be brought onboard the ship to sniff around, and you'll face stiff penalties if even a small amount of illegal drugs is found in your cabin. As a side note, if you're a drug-runner at home, that's not the carry-on bag to bring on the cruise ship.

Also, if you try to bring marijuana back into the US, even from St. Thomas and Puerto Rico, which fall under U.S. jurisdiction, you could be charged with drug trafficking. Pleading, "But it's legal at home" won't save you.

Crimes on ships rarely go unnoticed. Security cameras are almost everywhere, minus bathroom, the spa treatment rooms, and inside staterooms.

On a recent cruise, our neighbors told us this story: They purchased a bottle of very expensive Chilean wine in port, and asked their steward to chill it for them. She set it on her cleaning cart in the hallway while she went to get ice, around the corner. Although she returned less than a minute later, the wine was gone.

Ship Security was called, and they combed through the camera feed from the corridor. Using facial recognition software, they promptly identified the thieves, and made their way to their cabin. The couple initially denied taking any wine, but when confronted with a printed photo of them gleefully swiping the bottle, they had nothing to say. I watched them in the next port, being summarily escorted off the ship, with luggage and sad faces.

The wine? Intact.

The vacation? Not so much.

What About Ship-Wide Problems?

A ship sinks, another runs aground, the Bermuda Triangle eats one whole? Tragedies at sea are very rare, almost as unheard-of as a UFO landing for a picnic on your roof. Bottom line: you're going to be fine. If not, you'll have a great story to tell. The past few years have seen some high profile and tragic incidents, including onboard fires on Oceania *Insignia,* Royal Caribbean's *Grandeur of the Seas* and Carnival *Triumph,* and the capsizing of Costa *Concordia.* You heard about them only because they're uncommon; that's why they make the evening news. You're taking a bigger risk driving to the airport or boarding a plane to get to your homeport than you are once at sea. I count worrying as one of my talents, but I don't worry about cruising one bit.

There are strict international maritime laws that all cruise ships obey. Cruise ships that sail in U.S. waters are regularly inspected by the U.S. Coast Guard for any irregularities or safety issues that might be of concern. All cruise ships, regardless of where they sail, operate under international rules, known as Safety of Life at Sea (SOLAS), which regulate everything from fire safety to navigation and maritime security. Staff and crew take safety seriously!

The main reason you'll attend the mandatory muster drill on the first day of every cruise is to review the safety precautions onboard. It's also muscle-memory; if you pay attention, you'll know where to go in an emergency. The location is also printed in bold on your plastic key card.

Big events, like sinking or running aground, hardly ever occur. Nevertheless, like the Boy Scouts, be prepared.

You should know how to behave in a crisis, even though they're unlikely. Screaming, running around in circles, and berating crew members is less effective than calmly listening and following instructions. Keeping a sense of humor will help, although you may wish to avoid Titanic jokes.

In any emergency or scary situation, think of the children. With their limited life experience, they can really freak out, especially if things are crashing around them. Move calmly, speak carefully. Take a minute to reassure nearby young ones, yours or others. A smile or wink across the room can calm a frightened child before they totally wind up; if the Big People are not afraid, it must be okay. Take care not to project your fears onto a child. It's likely the worst case scenario that's scaring you spit-less isn't even on their young radar. All a child needs to know is that the adults are in charge and all will be well, even if there's an adventure along the way.

As we flew to Disneyworld, the plane hit sudden turbulence, the kind that dropped it several hundred feet in one fell swoop. Around us, adult passengers screamed and sobbed, while reaching for airsickness bags. I turned to our five-year-old daughter to comfort her. I was startled to see her grinning, eyes alight, arms over her head, very quietly mouthing "Wheeee–!" She giggled, "You said there will be roller coasters at Disneyworld. I'm *practicing!*"

In very rough seas, loose items can fly around. In your cabin, if things start to slide, do what you can to keep yourself safe. Place heavier objects on the floor, and small items such as toiletries in the sink or a drawer. You may have already noticed that the beds are pretty much the only movable furniture in the cabin. Televisions are secured, the cabinets are built in, and the tables are weighted to prevent sliding. In a bad storm, your water bottle may slide off the table, but the desk will not move.

In public areas, heavy items such as couches and planters are anchored firmly, but in very high seas, plates and glassware can go flying. If the ship is rolling hard, don't go to the bar where the chairs and tables and maybe the piano are sliding from side-to-side. This is another good reason to wear closed-toed shoes in rough weather; those cute flip flops are worthless for walking through broken glass.

Did you know a fire is the biggest danger at sea? On nearly every cruise, you'll see crew members practicing fire control. Or maybe not; they often do drills on port days, when most passengers are out and about. Fire spreads fast, and even on a ship surrounded by water, it's hard to put it out. That's why candles and other flammable items are not allowed on ships, and why smoking areas are regulated. Even a tiny cigarette butt, tossed carelessly overboard, can be blown back onto the ship. If it lands in your neighbor's towel drying on a nearby balcony, it's a sudden problem!

Real crises, like a sinking ship, are extremely unlikely, but storms at sea are pretty common. The captain will skirt them as best as possible, but sometimes, *through* is the only way to get where the ship is going. Avoid the upper open deck in high winds; fifty knot winds can whip you off your feet or even throw you overboard. Besides, stiff winds hurt, scouring bare skin better than any dermabrasion treatment in the spa.

Often, outer decks will be closed in very rough seas for safety. If winds are fiercesome on one side of the ship, outer doors on that side may be roped off to prevent doors slamming, as well as passengers going airborne. Those doors are very heavy, and with the push of an angry wind, they can be dangerous. You'd be more comfortable staying put if winds get very high, but if you need to get around, use the handrails, and avoid elevators.

There, you're warned, but please bear in mind, at this very minute, 300,000 humans are on cruise ships all around the world, and they'll be just fine. So will you.

Staying Safe While In Port

Crimes can occur anywhere, but face it, they usually don't. Most of us go years between being a victim, if ever. If you are going to be a crime victim while on a cruise, it's most likely to occur when you are ashore. Most crimes committed against cruise passengers are those of opportunity, such as petty theft or pickpockets, which can usually be avoided. Bad Guys know you'll only be in port a few hours or a day, and you won't want to waste precious time filling out paperwork at the local police station. Thieves strike fast, and are gone.

The key is to make yourself less of a target. Don't put your wallet in a back pocket; if someone gets into your front pants pocket, I guarantee you'll notice. If you carry a purse, tote bag or, backpack, be sure to carry it in front when in crowded areas (buses, subways, trains, elevators, or busy streets). Make sure they're zipped closed. Running a simple safety pin through the closure will slow down a sneaky hand in your bag. A skilled pickpocket won't waste those few extra seconds, risking notice. I've seen cameras snatched right off those annoying little selfie sticks, so keep a tight grip.

Jewelry rule of thumb– if you can't imagine living without your grandmother's wedding ring or your expensive Cartier watch, it's best to leave it at home. You may think you look like an icon of style, but to criminals and con-artists you appear as an icon of opportunity. It's also wise not to look like a million bucks if you're trying to bargain with the locals, and sparkly jewelry may set you apart from other folks on the street when you're trying to blend in.

Most people on the planet are decent, good-hearted souls, going about their daily lives. Fearing travel is limiting, as well as pathetic. Common sense is a good idea, wherever you go. In higher-risk areas, you might be safer on a tour, whether a private one or even through the cruise line's excursion department. A local guide can steer clear of risks you may not even notice. I was uneasy when we visited Istanbul, and knowing our local guide had our backs was a comfort. Turns out my fears were justified: most cruise lines cancelled all of their ports in Turkey through 2017 at least.

Just as you'd avoid sketchy areas at home, or when visiting domestic cities, stay out of rough areas on a cruise, too. You're always better off with others, either family, traveling companions, or a tour group, rather than walking alone in foreign places. Plus, should an adventure befall you, good or bad, you'll have a witness to corroborate your story.

On your own or on a tour, walk purposefully, as if you know where you're going. Don't be the lost sheep wandering aimlessly, an easy target for any potential wolves. If you need to consult a map, or guidebook, do it somewhere private, not on a street corner. Recognize you'll still stand out as Not From Around Here, no matter what you do, but at least make an effort to look confident.

Try to blend in as much as possible. If you're from rural Oklahoma, the minute you open your mouth, everyone will know you're a tourist. Actually, American travelers can be spotted *before* they speak, by the way they dress, move, act, carry themselves. Dress is a big giveaway. Americans tend to be more casual than other places. For example, in Europe, only people actually physically exercising wear workout clothes such as tank tops, shorts, tee shirts. They don't dress like that on the streets. You know across North America, that's practically a uniform. Europeans wear real shoes, not the running shoes many Americans favor, just about everywhere; again, they'd change footwear at the gym if they planned to work out.

Walking while your face is buried in your screen is not only likely to lead you smack into posts, but you need to be aware of your surroundings and people around you. Plus, you're missing the place, which is why you came, remember?

Be very aware of your surroundings. If you see something that seems "off," like a guy wearing a thick black parka in a Caribbean airport or head-to-toe camo in the market, trust your gut. Simply move to another area. We live in serious times. Don't walk in fear, but staying off the evening news is a worthy goal.

Stories about The Ugly Tourists abound, but the stories that leave locals thinking, "They're just like us! Who knew!" are much better. Don't mock local customs or dress, and stop complaining about things being different than your home base. Of course, it's not the same! If it was just like home, you wouldn't bother going to a new place at all.

As I tell the grandkids when they wrinkle their little noses, "Different does not mean bad."

I also say "Pay attention. You might learn something." And "Wash your hands. You don't know where they've been."

As a grandmother, it's in my job description to dispense wisdom.

Food, Food, Everywhere Is Food!

You'd have to make a conscious effort to go hungry on a cruise ship. You could be like my niece, who only eats white foods; no parsley on her naked noodles, no meat or berries or cheese, or, heaven forbid, anything green. For the rest of us, choices abound.

First, let's talk about restaurants at sea. Of course, venues vary by the ship, but all will have some sort of a main dining room, and at least one casual eatery. Most have much more. Some of the newest ships have over a dozen restaurants on board, not including snack-places and room service. Most are part of your cruise charges, while the fancier places have a cover charge. If you go hungry, it's your own fault.

In the spirit of being the best-informed person onboard, read your daily schedule for food tips you'd otherwise miss. Did you know NCL will deliver a hot pizza anywhere on the ship for $5 any time of the day or night? Yes, anywhere, including the pool area, the promenade deck, the third aisle back in the theater, and the casino. Expect to get odd looks if you order pizza delivered to a spinning class in the workout center.

Breakfast and Lunch:

Personally, I'd rather sleep an extra twenty minutes than eat breakfast food. At home, my default breakfast menu is often leftover last night's dinner, and it's hours after I get up. I think facing squishy foods like pancakes, oatmeal, and eggs is a lousy way to greet the day. However, I recognize many people disagree with me, including Husband, whose favorite meal is breakfast. We've been married a long time, but we're still not compatible, especially culinarily speaking.

Room service can be a good option for breakfast. Order the night before, and it'll be delivered to your cabin around the time you request, give or take a little. On most cruise lines, they'll call ahead to remind you it's on the way. It's a pleasant wake-up call, not to mention a chance for you to grab some clothes. Nobody wants to see that, trust me. Or, throw on some clothes and head to the main dining room or buffet.

Usually, Husband gets up and eagerly sets off to find his breakfast, while I leisurely start my day. I guess he gets lonely. On our last cruise, Husband thought the way to convert me to his way of thinking was to have breakfast on our balcony. The advantage, from my point of view, was twofold: he'd quit badgering me, and I could just roll out of bed. Plus, eating overlooking the sea sounded romantic.

It may have been, had the food been better, or at least edible. Husband went a little nuts in the ordering: eggs, French toast, fruit, sausage, hash browns, the whole thing. Lukewarm scrambled eggs that had obviously had a bad experience, including a recent run in with an ice cream scoop, French toast too dry to bite, cold sausage, miniature doorstops disguised as hash brown triangles, and room temperature milk cartons ... Ugh! The only item I could eat was the banana, which came instead of the offered fruit cup on the menu. Just as well; bananas are more reliable. The experience didn't convert me to breakfast food.

That was an anomaly; usually, room service is not a bad option. For a bedtime snack, it can't be beat.

As I was saying before I digressed, yes, you can head for the buffet or main dining room for your morning meal. Breakfast in the main dining room is always open seating. It's a fine way to meet new people, if your eyes are open enough for a chat that time of day. Full service breakfast takes longer than other venues, but it offers a more upscale menu and solicitous waiters delivering juice and pastry while your food cooks. And you're less likely to get stepped on by that guy hell-bent on getting a slice of French toast, not caring that there's plenty more where that came from.

The buffet can be chaotic at busy times, but it's fast, you can pick and choose on the spot, and the variety of food is usually good. If you need a quick meal on a port day before your tour, this might be your best option. Why wait for full service if all you want is hot cocoa and yogurt? Grab that and be on your way.

Seek out undercover breakfasts; you're not limited to the dining room and buffet. Onboard coffee cafés offer pastries and fresh fruit, sometimes breakfast sandwiches, and you don't need to purchase a fancy drink; the food is free. Some ships have a small café by the pool or spa. They often offer a limited variety of breakfast items, without the commotion of the buffet.

Keep that in mind for later in the day, too. While the cafés usually charge for the fancy coffees, the pretty pastries and snacks are free for the asking. Those mini sandwiches, paninis, salads, macaroons, quiche and tall layer cakes might be better than lunch, some days. Feel free to take a plate of cheesecake-on-a-stick with you to the pool deck, or a heap of cowboy cookies back to your cabin to read. Food and drinks are allowed pretty much anywhere on the ship, except the library and restrooms. Eeeewww; did I need to say that?

Lunch can be a quick slice of pizza or a hot dog by the pool, a heap of salad from the buffet, a sit down in the dining room. You might scope out the burger joint. On some ships, the specialty restaurants are open for lunch, for a lesser fee than dinner. On Royal Caribbean, the dining room only serves lunch on sea days.

Often, a pop-up venue appears on sea days, maybe a German grill on Deck Fourteen, a low-country fish boil, or a Caribbean feast on the pool deck. Pho in the sports bar, high tea (one day only), paella on the promenade, even a jazz brunch or a mystery dinner may be offered. Watch for hands-on experiences, where you learn to make pasta, then sit down to a lovely Italian luncheon.

Some one-time dining events are easily missed if you're not on the lookout. Do a little research before you board, study the daily agenda left in your cabin each night, or ask on your first day about special offerings during the cruise.

Dinner

Dinner time varies with the cruise line or ship. There are three possibilities: early seating (about 6:00 pm), late seating (about 8:00-8:30 pm) or open seating (anytime within a given time frame, like 5:30-9:30).

Early seating might mean you'd have to rush for dinner if you are on a shore excursion that lasts until the late afternoon, or can't tear yourself away from the beach or pool. On the other hand, early seating allows you to go to the shows after dinner and have more time for nightlife before bed. I prefer dinner-and-a-show rather than the reverse, although early dining can be too early some days.

Late seating allows you to have plenty of time to get ready for dinner. However, if you don't finish dinner until after 10:00 pm, you might either miss the show or part of the night life. Not to mention your poor digestive system! If you get heartburn from eating so much that late, I don't want to hear about it.

On Norwegian Cruise Line, open seating is the only option. NCL pioneered the concept, and they do it very well. Some variation of open seating is available on almost all cruise lines, or a mixture of both fixed seating and open seating. Open seating is like any land-based restaurant; you show up, you may have a brief wait, they seat you, you dine. If this appeals most to you, speak up when you're booking the cruise.

Specialty restaurants are another option. I love choices, don't you? Extra-fee venues offer gourmet foods, a calmer ambiance, or a theme. Steakhouse, Asian, Mexican, Italian, Brazilian steakhouse, teppanyaki, or eateries serving menus designed by famous chefs are some of the choices. Obviously, it varies by ship, along with the cover charge.

Smart cruisers know a few ways around the specialty restaurant's extra fees. Try asking your travel agent for a free dinner when you book; it's a common perk. Loyalty programs almost always include upscale dinner or two. On some cruises, we've had so many free specialty dinners, we hardly saw the main dining room. See if your cruise offers lunch in a specialty restaurant, when the cover charge is less for a very similar menu. Often, on embarkation night, if the fancy restaurants are not fully booked, the ship will often offer two-for-one, a free bottle of wine, or other incentive.

Several cruise lines offer specialty dining packages, which allow you to pay a reduced rate for multiple restaurant reservations on a cruise. Read the fine print to ensure the package works for you, because the cruise line stipulates which restaurants and how many reservations in each. If you are like Husband, who detests Asian food and can't figure out how 1.3 billion people say alive eating 'that stuff," you're wasting money on a dining package that includes two nights at the onboard Asian fusion restaurant. In that case, you're better off just booking the steakhouse, singly.

Even in the main dining room, have a little sense of adventure! A steak and baked potato can be had anywhere, but can you get creamed frog legs at home? Expand your horizons. Now's your chance to try duck confit, dragon fruit, beef carpaccio, even salmon tartare. I must caution you about the salmon, however: that's pronounced tarTAR, not tarTER. One's raw fish, the other a common mayo-based condiment, not necessarily interchangeable.

Room Service is generally free, except for service charges on certain lines in the middle of the night. Royal Caribbean's late-night orders bear a $3.95 fee, while all orders on Norwegian cost $7.95, midnight-5 a.m. Tipping is recommended, but in-room dining is not the splurge it would be at a hotel.

If I remember at home, I make up tips for room service by rubber-banding a couple of dollars around a candy bar. Seeing the server's face light up is fun, and I think it improves service the next time I order. If you plan to tip for room service, you'd better have it in hand when the knock comes at the door. The servers are as quick as hummingbirds, with no time for you root through a drawer looking for a couple bucks.

Room service menus are rather limited. You might be better off scouting out a midday snack yourself, rather than hanging around, waiting for delivery. Food can be carried just about anywhere, as can drinks. If you find the buffet too hectic, feel free to take a plate to a lounge, by the pool, to your cabin. For anything bigger than a few cookies or apple, ask a crew member for a cloche to cover your plate, and you're on your way.

Buffet

I know mothers around the world teach their little ones manners, but all that seems to go out the windows at buffets, and kids are not the worst offenders. Seriously, I've seen people stampede to get to a basket of pretzel rolls, or push others aside in the ice cream line. I've also witnessed some acts that make me queasy, like the man licking his fingers in the buffet line, and the woman who bit a sandwich, then set it back on the tray. If you're smart enough to read my book, I suspect I'm preachin' to the choir here, but humor me as I review some basic buffet etiquette. And if your own mama failed in her duties, here's a run-down:

First, take a breath. There are third-world countries that have less food stockpiled than a cruise ship. If you have to wait a few seconds longer, you're not going to go hungry. Even in a worst-case scenario, such as getting to the buffet twelve minutes after it closes, you're still going to be just fine. A well-known Scout truism says, "It's biologically impossible for a kid to starve to death on an overnight campout." It's unlikely you'll die, if you refrain from trampling other passengers. The food on your plate isn't going anywhere either, so please wait until you're seated to chomp your burger.

It's smart to narrow down a seating location when entering, so your party can meet up after you all get your meal. Agreeing to meet "port side, halfway back" beats yodeling through the ship. I'm telling you, I've heard actual yodeling in the buffet. Or else someone named their kid something with a whole lot of vowels in it.

While you're looking around, figure out the choreography of the buffet. They usually only go in one direction, even the Action Stations set up on some ships. Going upstream is both annoying and inefficient.

You wouldn't cut the line at the grocery store, so don't do it on a cruise ship. Even when someone is lollygagging, try to wait patiently. If you're the slow one, keep in mind there's an entire line of people behind you, also hoping to eat lunch at some point. If the section ahead of you doesn't appeal to you (you're not interested in salads), it's okay to slip out of line, but don't barge back in further along. You're a nice person, remember?

If you forget a small item, such as a roll, or a slice of cheese, it's fine to take it without waiting in the line, but be polite: ask if you can grab the item, preferably without knocking down the line of people like a row of dominoes. "Excuse me, I just need a roll" is courteous.

I like kids, better than most grown-ups some days, but steam will come out of both ears if you let your little ones run amok in a buffet. Your main job as a parent is to teach these young people, so they will grow into civilized adults. Yes, even on vacation. A buffet is a prime venue for talking about not grabbing food with bare hands, taking the one you touched first, and so forth. Smaller kids also need to be reminded not to run around and risk knocking over people carrying trays or drinks.

Speaking of fingers, kids aren't the only offenders here. Adults are just as likely to grab the top cucumber or the front drumstick with their hands, or root around for the best bit of fish, even if it's on the bottom of the platter. Don't do it. Use the tongs or spoons, even for awkward items like cheese slices.

Oh, those tongs: never, ever move the serving utensils from one platter to another. What if the person behind you has allergies to shrimp and you've just moved a spoon from a shrimp dish to a chicken dish? What if somebody is vegetarian, and doesn't want beef stew on their spinach? What if ...? Look, just don't do it. If you need another serving utensil, ask a crew member to bring you another. They tend to hover in buffets. The crew, not the tongs.

Remember to grab a clean plate if you go back for seconds. You're not the one washing dishes, so you don't have to economize to the point of germ-spreading. Leave your used plate at the table. If the crew is on the ball, it will magically vanish while you're getting more noodles.

Invite others to sit, if there are a couple of empty chairs at your table. Sharing tables is common in Europe, but Americans might not think to ask. Husband and I make a point of saying, "There are seats here," if we see people wandering around with full plates of food. Who knows, you might make a new buddy, or learn something. Seats are always limited; don't be those people who spread out across a six-top, blocking others from sitting at all. Safe conversation starters: Is this your first cruise? Did you see the desserts? What are your plans for tomorrow's port?

Main Dining Room

At home, I often begin to consider tonight's menu about an hour before dinner time, as in "Hmm, wonder what's for dinner tonight?" Cruise ships are more on top of the game, no surprise there. If you're interested in details, be sure to read the BONUS excerpt from my book, *Mediterranean Cruise*, in the back of this one. I'll include a ship's shopping list, and detail how they prepare 10,000 meals a day.

Did you know that all of the main dining room meals are planned months ahead, and you can look at menus in advance? Just visit the Guest Services desk and ask to see the menu for each night of your cruise. You can decide which nights you want to stick to main dining room dining, and when you would rather spring for an alternative restaurant, or graze the buffet.

In most cases, you can even check out the menus online before the cruise. The menus on mainstream cruises rotate on a predictable schedule, with few changes. Do a search. Type in the name of ship, name of the specialty restaurant (or main dining room), and menu. Check to be sure the listing is recent.

Weight Gain Is Not Inevitable!

Everything you've heard about 24 hour food is true, but you're not obligated to eat all of it. If you cruise mainly to eat (and eat, and eat) you can find ways to consume 6,000+ calories in one sea day, put your body into overdrive from excessive sugar intake, and swell your feet with salt levels that rival the Dead Sea. You *can*, but there's no need to eat any more recklessly than at home. In fact, I highly recommend you avoid eating yourself into a stupor. You'll feel better, and hey, there's always more tomorrow.

As anywhere else, having a few smart strategies regarding what to put on your plate makes reasonable eating more, well, reasonable. I suggest having a plan in mind before you face down that loooong dessert display. They're prettier than they taste, anyway. The general advice: be mindful. Think about what you're ordering or picking out at the buffet. At home, you probably wouldn't eat the ribs, steak, fish *and* chicken all at one meal, would you? If you want to sample it all, at least keep the portions sample-sized. If your waistbands hurt mid-cruise, don't come crying to me.

Think about portion size. Consider sharing the melting chocolate cake with ooey-gooey caramel sauce and pecans with a friend. Order two appetizers instead of the entrée, if it looks good. And don't lick your plate; the first bites taste best.

Increase the vegetables and fruits in your diet onboard. Besides being good for you, they'll fill you up better than macaroni and cheese. By the way, contrary to what Husband insists, french fries are not vegetables, nor are dill pickles. They're just not. Eating melons, oats, and herbs will help your body deal with more salt than you probably eat at home. They're natural diuretics, and available on any ship.

I routinely order extra vegetables at dinner. Three carrot slices does not a serving make, in my opinion, even next to one turnip cube. This tactic worked great, up until our most recent cruise. My request was met by a bowl of plain steamed broccoli, every single evening! After Day Three, I understood why President George H Bush hated broccoli. By Day Eight, I couldn't even look at the stuff. By Day Twelve, I was queasy just thinking about broccoli, but there was no turning back. Come to think of it, I haven't bought broccoli since we returned from that trip.

Everyone talks about how you can order three main courses or two desserts on a cruise ship dinner– and you can! Or order three entrees for the two of you and share, just to get a taste. I'm a big fan of crab cakes. When they're on the menu, I'll order a triple serving and call it dinner.

Fewer people mention that you can also ask for half-portions of most menu items. If you want to sample rich fare, but know you don't have the willpower to stop at a few bites, order a smaller portion. Ask for half-portions of entrees, either *as* an entrée, or for an appetizer. That creamy shrimp Alfredo sauce has more calories than a triple hot fudge mega sundae, but a half portion ... go for it.

Obviously, this technique doesn't work with a T-bone steak, but with easily-divisible items like pasta, vegs, or risotto, no one will raise an eyebrow. Also, unless your mom is traveling with you, no one will scold you for not cleaning your plate. It becomes a spelling issue: would you prefer the food go to *waste,* or to *waist?*

You know you can jump all over the menu, right? Don't be like a spoiled family member who demanded a cheeseburger in the main dining room, insisting the poor waiter run up six stories to acquire one from the poolside grill. But if it's anywhere on the menu, feel free to mix and match. You can certainly have noodles with the fish, or baked potatoes with the chicken, if you wish.

Oh, that reminds me: if you love love love something but it's not on the menu, go ahead and ask if it's available. Use your manners, of course. The ship almost always has shrimp, baked potatoes, and other things not shown on a daily basis. Customizing is one of the perks of a vacation at sea.

A tablemate on a recent cruise was in the middle of chemotherapy. Also, in the middle of the wide Atlantic ocean, which seemed unwise to me, but she was bound and determined to enjoy this long-planned cruise with her mother and brother. Anyway, her appetite was very low. The only thing that appealed to her was plain shrimp, and peaches. After the first night, our sweet waiter made sure our table had plates of both, whether or not she felt up to coming to dinner that day.

Most ships will not advertise this, but you can get cheese and crackers and a fresh sliced fruit plate at the main dining room every night. Just ask. Also, every dessert menu I've ever read has a cheese plate, with fancy cheeses, dried fruits, grapes, nuts. Feel free to order this for an appetizer, even if it's listed as a dessert.

Or order off the children's menu, if you'd like. Personally, I raised our kids to eat what the rest of us eat, but the kid menus have comfort foods you might not find elsewhere, and they come in child-friendly portions. If you're craving a grilled cheese or unidentifiable nuggets, go ahead and order them. Desserts are less fussy on the children's menu, too; a brownie and ice cream over a mocha parfait, for instance.

Don't be bullied into ordering every course in the dining room, unless you want to. The waiters want you to leave a good review–their jobs depend on it–so they tend to do whatever it takes to make you happy. In our society, that can take the form of plying you with more food than Grandma. We've had waiters bring un-ordered plates, and others who tried to talk us into ordering all four appetizers, "just to taste; I think you'll love it." Last cruise, the waiter never brought a dessert menu to our table. Instead, he delivered one of each dessert, urged us to share and try them all, then order the one(s) we liked best. Sure, you can resist dessert, but it's tougher when the spoon's in your hand!

Pace Yourself at The Buffet

Indian food! Pasta with four sauces! Grilled meats! Beautiful cakes! It's tempting to pile your plate high with everything in front of you, then dig in until you're past the point of stuffed ... and more than a little queasy from chasing a third quesadilla with Asian stir-fry.

People tend to go a little berserk at a buffet, as if they haven't eaten in weeks and had better stock up while they have the chance. Many people are polite; others will step on toes and grab spoons in an effort to heap their plate to daredevil heights. Not saying you're one of them, but if the all-you-can-eat nature of a buffet frazzles you into overeating, you might be better off sticking with the main dining room for meals. Descriptions on paper are less appealing than a full-platter display under bright lights.

Or just make up your mind what you'll eat before you walk in: a heaping green salad, a protein, vegetables, one of those fabulous rolls, and two small 'treat' items, for example; then stick to the plan. If your mind is set before you see the spread, you can more easily dodge the temptation of that extra dessert. Or three.

Another tried-and-true tactic for not gorging on cruise ships is to mix up heavy and light meals. Planning to live it up with a Flintstone-sized steak at a specialty dining venue for dinner? Have a salad for lunch. Want to go all-out with a pancake, heaped omelet, and half pound of bacon breakfast feast? Order a simple fish dish for lunch, and skip the dessert.

A nephew routinely skips lunch on cruise ships, convinced dinner offerings are more appealing anyway. I'm not a fan of breakfast food: close to a thousand calories saved there alone. If you pair a splurge meal with lighter dining the rest of the day, your pants are less likely to dig in by mid-cruise. On the flip side, don't starve yourself, or that platter of warm cookies just set down in the atrium won't stand a chance.

Be Friendly!

Americans are really lousy at relaxing. You're probably drowning under undone projects, nagging chores, a tight schedule, and a To Do list that threatens to crush the light out of you. We don't even use up our meager vacation allotment, and we certainly don't pull the drapes for a month off, as do other places. No other country on earth puts as much time and money and magazine articles into figuring out how to unwind.

I'm baffled by people who spend months planning a cruise vacation and neglect to remember to lighten up once they're onboard! I like words, and the root word of "Vacation" is "Vacate." Leave it all behind–as much as you can!

On a ship, the only other people onboard, other than employees, are on vacation, out to have a good time. Join them! Nudge yourself out of the head-down-get-through-the-day mode. Be friendly, reach out, talk to people! Even in the first couple of hours, even in line before you board, smile and greet people. By the very fact that there you both stand, you already have some things in common. Where are you from, how was your trip to the ship, is this your first cruise, are you as excited as I am? are all valid conversation starters.

Don't wait for someone to be friendly to you first. If you start the cycle, it will snowball, and your time waiting in the Customs line will pass pleasantly. Of course, snobs abound; you may have the bad luck to bump into a 'Negative Nellie' or 'Grouchy Gregory.' I just say to myself, "Whew,

I'm glad I don't have to share a cabin with them," and turn to someone else. By far, most passengers are wonderful people!

I've found people nearly always respond positively, when offered a friendly greeting and a smile. Plus, you never know who you might meet. I had a funny experience on cruise to Europe, in reverse. We were playing cards one afternoon with a few couples we'd met onboard. Frank told us about a wonderful book he'd read; said he'd read it three times, and recommended it to everyone he knew. Husband shot me a glance. It was MY book. Husband didn't hesitate to introduce me as the author.

Frank yelled across the lounge, "Hey, Honey! That book I keep telling you about– *Mediterranean Cruise*–this is the author, the Cruise Addict's Wife *right here!*"

Then he turned to Husband. "You didn't really eat tacos in Quincy Market, did you?"

Why, yes, he did.

I'm basically shy, preferring to fly under the radar. That ended right there; the rest of the trip, every time I passed Frank on the ship, he shouted, "Hey, everybody! Have you met Deb? She wrote the *best* book about cruises!"

As we came into a port, I happened to ask about Frank's plan for the day. He admitted he had none, so I invited him to join us on a walking tour. His eyes lit up like Christmas. That whole morning, he pelted me with questions, in between quoting from my own book." Flattering, of course, but disconcerting as well.

Onboard, get involved. You're not at home, you'll never see these people again after next week, so let your inner child come out from behind the desk. Don't think that participating in what sounds like silly games on board is "for other people to do". Jump into the music trivia, or matches game, or whatever other activity is going on in the lounge. Get out of the sun for a few minutes on a sea day and share some laughs with other cruisers. I've met some of the most interesting folks on board, people I'd never encounter any other place, just by saying Hello. I had a great conversation with a 101-year-old WWI vet, traveling solo. I love a good storyteller.

Scan your daily schedule for new things to try. Expand your mind, rest your body, be someone new entirely, if you wish. If someone invites you to join them on their way to a photography lecture, be open minded. If you see a Pictionary team that needs three more players, introduce yourself. You can even try karaoke, if the inkling strikes. Step out of your routine–that's why you're on vacation.

Crew and Staff

The crew on a cruise ship deals with hundreds of people, all kinds and shapes, week after week. You'd be surprised to learn how long they work, day after day, months at a time. Their free time is measured in "hours" off, not "days" off. On top of an already hard job, I've seen passengers treat well-meaning crew disdainfully, as if they were furniture, not worthy of a second glance. You're better than that.

Take a moment to speak to a crew member; ask where they're from, family, how long is their contract, etc., treat them like people, not furniture. At the very least, smile (with eye contact!) at every crew or staff member you meet. Besides being polite, it'll benefit you in ways you'll miss if you strut by, nose in the air.

If you're friendly and approachable, they're more likely to be extra good to you. Ask your room steward or waiter for advice on shore; where's a free internet spot, or the best place to shop. They know more than you do! How else will you hear about the free shuttle to the center of town, or that quirky little headhunter museum?

Your cabin steward is often an untapped resource, and if you treat them nicely, they'll do just about anything reasonable to make your vacation even better. Need something? Ask! For example, the number one item left behind in hotels in America is cell phone chargers. In Europe, it's currency converters, probably the kind American use to charge their cell phones. On ships, it's wire hangers and hand-held luggage scales. If you need more hangers, forgot your charger, wish you had a lime, need more ice, or another blanket, or a box of tissue on the bedside table, ask!

Especially on lazy sea days, starting a brief conversation with any member of the staff can be an experience in itself. They're normally very friendly and willing to share where they're from and tell you about their families and their lives in faraway countries and islands. For the most part, they *like* people; otherwise, they'd have gone into the pathology profession, where conversation is limited.

A Cruise Director on one ship figured out our group's chosen meeting spot on port days, and made a point of stopping by daily. He'd ask what we had planned, and even gave us a head start at getting off the ship through the crew gangway. I'm sure it's because we spoke to him in a friendly manner that first day. One cabin steward made it a quest to find me each morning with a weather report, often in the form of "Your blouse is lovely, but grab a light jacket," or "Hot day today! You have your hat?"

The best advice was given by a smiley steward in Hawaii. She ventured "May I suggest ...?" She told us to walk 300 feet past the ship, around the fence, and look down into the water. Dozens of giant sea turtles, the honu, were roiling and mating in the warm water discharged from the electric plant. Those honu became the basis of my novel, *Peril in Paradise,* about a cruise to Hawaii. Do you know how much money I've made from that novel because that steward felt free to offer a friendly comment? Had I been brusque, she would not have bothered telling me about the turtles at all.

The day before Sitka, a member of the Activities staff asked me if I planned to go to the New Archangel Dancers performance in port. I hadn't heard of them, but I was willing to listen. Turned out to be a fun half hour show. They're an all-women dance troupe which performs Russian folk dances, only when a cruise ship is in port. We'd have missed out, had I not listened.

In my experience, I've met passengers who treat their stewards like a servant, not worthy of a glance. My parents taught me better, and as a result, stewards have gone out of their way to help me, and I mean *way* out of their way! A steward in Tortola told me about a slave museum in port that I found fascinating, another gave me the port's Wi-Fi password so I could catch up on email, a few have suggested hidden spots on the ship where I could write by a big window, undisturbed. Others have brought us extra treats, whimsical towel animals to make us smile, on and on.

Be friendly, but keep in mind: you are on vacation, they are not. Sure, crew members enjoy talking with travelers, and they especially enjoy little children, since they might not see their own family for up to nine months in a stretch. By all means, be pleasant to them–but be respectful of their time. I've heard of many passengers who befriend crew members on Facebook, bring them t shirts and perfume from their hometown, totally forgetting they really have nothing in common, short of being on the same ship at the same time. Talk to them, greet them, be friendly and non-demanding; just don't plan on a long term relationship. They may love you, but next cruise, you'll be replaced by someone else in the same cabin, and they will love them, too.

Ask a Local

No one knows your hometown as well as somebody who lives there, and that's true, worldwide. Most people are happy to recommend a site you shouldn't miss, or a great restaurant that tourists never frequent. Some of our best travel memories were triggered by asking, "It's our first time here; what should we not miss?"

Talk to shopkeepers and taxi drivers, tour guides, those people at the crosswalk, and restaurant servers. They know more, just because they live there. Exception: In Alaska, most store clerks are imported from the Lower 48 for the cruise season. Many are college students. At the end of September, shops shutter and close, and the towns return to their delicious small-ness.

Pelt locals with questions; real questions are the way to gain insight into the area. That's why you're there, remember? As we've traveled, especially out of North America, we make a point of asking our tour drivers about education, military service, women, family structure, religion, what's the area famous for, and we respectfully ask, "What do you want us to see?" Once they recognize we're genuinely interested, we learn all kinds of stuff that enriches our vacation. Usually, tour operators genuinely like people, and are anxious to share information they have.

For example, we talked to our tour guide in Turkey, and once we convinced him we actually cared, he warmed up. While Turkey is officially 98% Muslim, he said less than 40% are 'practicing.' He admitted the locals were worried about the two thousand refugees in their area. Since then, hundreds of thousands have flooded that city, and I've wondered how he's faring.

Unemployment rates in Naples (the guide insisted, "*Napoli*! Naples is in Florida") are listed at 53%, but our driver confided he knew *two* people with full-time jobs, both government workers. The driver himself had two master's degrees, in math and engineering, but could not find work in his field. A driver in Greece told us about the dire economy and corrupt local politics, then asked, "What's up with JLo, anyway?" Where else can you get that perspective?

We attended a performance of the melodrama "Days Of '98" In Skagway, Alaska, then lingered to speak to the lead actor. He was also the town's high school math teacher. Fascinating! He told us the small communities in Alaska are linked by video-chat. Students can participate in class discussions, even if they're the only student in town. He said the oil industry's money made Alaska's schools technologically advanced, to the point where students who transfer to the Lower 48 are often a couple of years ahead of their peers. I didn't know that!

In Barbados, we asked what the area was famous for, and did it have anything to do with that delicious warm molasses aroma wafting over the pier? Our guide said that sugar was the major—and only!– export. *One hundred percent* of the sugar produced on the island was sent to Great Britain, per a century-old contract. He explained, "We must buy our table sugar from Mexico." 100%?! Whoever negotiated that deal?

A driver in Juneau, Alaska, raved about their governor, Sarah Palin. This was about a month before she was nominated to be vice president. He went on and on about how she had cleaned up corruption, cut down on waste by selling the state's private planes and firing the governor's mansion's chef, insisting on cooking for her own family.

"She has 80% approval rating!"

Eighty percent of the people agreed she was a great governor? Wow; it's tough to get 80% of any group to agree on anything, including what day of the week it is.

In Tortola –and other parts of the Caribbean— marriage is seen as a novelty. We met a young mother, and asked about her family. She was confused; she had no family structure, just these two adorable children in the buggy. Seeing our genuine interest, she explained most of the residents are descendants from slaves, and 'masters" discouraged family relationships. That cut down on weeping and wailing when parents and children and lovers were sold on down the river, so to speak. Decades later, families are fluid, and few marry, or expect relationships to last. The lack of permanence was unnerving to me.

Do you know about the Angels of the Mud in Florence, Italy? Simply asking "What else do you want us to know, to take home as a memory of your hometown?" netted a story that brought tears to my eyes.

Our private tour driver, Giovanni, related the story about the thousand-year-old National Library in Florence. It's on the banks of the Arno River. Forty-nine years ago, the river flooded severely, and a muddy torrent rushed into the first two stories. Residents to save the ancient books, sculptures, and paintings stored there. The Mayor drew his weapon and announced that anyone who came to the National Library to save merely old paintings and books would be shot on the spot. He insisted saving the city itself was more important than a bunch of old art and books.

A flood of young people came from the cities nearby, from the universities, overwhelming the Mayor. They formed a brigade, quickly passing out the ancient books and paintings and sculptures, then stayed to wash the mud from the eyes of the statues. They saved the treasures, and the townspeople were forever grateful. The young people were dubbed "Angelo de Fango," Angels of the Mud. Giovanni said with a derisive snort, "and the Mayor, we no longer speak his name."

In Greece, we asked, "What should we not miss?" and a man directed us to a bakery, which had been in constant operation since 1820. I had no idea that many kinds of baklava existed! Great heaps of neatly arranged pastries towered in glass cases, each better than its neighbors. We noticed a McDonald's down the block. I felt sad for the people standing in line outside the restaurant, missing these local delicacies baked by the team of scurrying bakers behind the counter.

I believe it's essential to Be Where You Are at all times, most importantly when traveling. If the only thing you can tell about your cruise when you return home is, "I sat on a beach. I drank some beer," in my mind, you could have stayed home. Nothing wrong with a good beach day, but at least know enough to keep your eye out for the sea creatures that frequent the area, be they giant sea turtles or tiny stinging jellyfish. As for the beer, I think knowing that very barstool was Hemingway's favorite adds to the experience. I'm not

saying you need to get a degree in history, but at least talk to
people who live there!

You need to *trust* the residents, too. I wanted liege
sugar in Denmark, a couple pounds, please. Liege sugar is
luscious pearlized sugar used in liege waffles and other
desserts, and it's not easy to find in America. We explored
downtown Copenhagen on foot for two days, and never saw a
food store. Finally, I turned to the hotel clerk.

She was baffled as to why I wanted sugar–don't they
sell sugar in America?–but assured me a market was not far.
"Go left two blocks, into the coffee shop, then down the
steps." I was baffled. I'd passed that coffee shop six times,
never seeing any indication of a market.

"Just walk," she nudged.

Reluctantly, we walked down the two blocks, into the
coffee shop, down the steps, and a grocery store lay before
me. It was the size of my living room, but well stocked and
interesting. While Husband hunted for treasures, I found the
tiny baking-supplies shelf, and strained to make out pictures,
since my Danish is non-existent. We made our purchases.

I knew there was no market: I'd been by there. She
knew there was a market; she'd experienced it. We need to
listen to those who are farther down the road, rather than
arguing, as is often our first impulse. If a local tells you the
very best shrimp on the island is in that ramshackle hut, or the
smaller waterfall is less crowded and more beautiful than the
advertised one, or you really need to see that museum, take
them at face value. It's quite possible they know more than
you do.

Oh, the sugar? Turned out to be desiccated coconut. Apparently my ability to guess at packaging is about as good as my Danish language skills. I ordered liege sugar online when I reached home. That's not the point, is it?

Online Roll Calls

Often passengers will "meet" online, and make plans to meet in person onboard the ship. CruiseCritics.com's roll calls are ideal for this, as are other websites. Look up the ship and date of your sailing, and in nearly every cruise, you'll find a group of chatty cruisers looking forward to the voyage every bit as much as you.

On a cruise with a set table assignment, roll calls can also be a link for making friends online, then dining together. Our upcoming cruise already set up a "friends and solos" dinner table, for single travelers and whoever else wishes to join them. Names taken, then the cruise line contacted to link dining reservations. It guarantees a solo or lonely passenger will have someone to sit with and talk to at dinner. Never a bad thing.

Roll calls are also a good way to fill up your private tour, or join someone else's. Often, private tours are priced by the vehicle, not per person. If you find a private tour for six, and your group has four, you can save money and meet new people by advertising to fill the van. We've had great fun with this kind of arrangement, and enjoyed spending a few hours with like-minded travelers. Arranging it all ahead of time makes the day so much smoother.

These groups often make plans for activities on board, months in advance–and all you have to do is show up. Our next cruise already has a board game time (bring your favorite game or a deck of cards, meet same time, same place, on every sea day), slot pull, cabin crawl (to show off the different levels of cabins), a group walking tour in one of the ports, ping pong tournaments, a book discussion group, a gift exchange (limit $10, something representative of your hometown), and I'm sure I forgot a few things.

For the craft hour, passengers are encouraged to bring whatever hand work they wish, and work on their own project while chatting with others. Crochet, knitting, even water colors are some of the interests. Personally, I'm not going to pack any extra bulk or weight. I don't think I could fit my garden or quilting frames in a suitcase, anyway.

Speaking of crafts on ships, I read an article a few years ago that rattled me. It was about a 106-day around-the-world cruise. Naturally, with many days at sea, passengers planned ahead and brought things to keep them occupied. The article was written by a woman to whom I grant the benefit of the doubt in assuming others might be bored. She was a knitter, and packed *cases* of extra knitting needles. Any "lonely" passenger she spotted "wasting time" relaxing, reading a novel, or basking in the sun, was coerced into learning how to knit socks. She insisted the long cruise be used to produce many socks to be donated to her favorite charity at home.

Apparently, she was ... let's say ... *persuasive*, because she went on to detail how excited all the passengers were, and how happy it made her feel to see so many heads bent over knitting needles during the evening shows and around the pool. By the second port, she even organized a field trip to find local yarns to resupply everyone. "No one was interested in old buildings and beaches anyway. The yarn shops were delightful!"

The article made me itch, and I don't mean from the scratchy yarn. The vision of a bossy passenger browbeating innocent travelers into taking up her obsession was painful even to read. She said "Everyone loved it." I doubt she counted the passengers who were quick enough to see her coming and duck. Go ahead, strike up a conversation with other passengers, but don't try to detour them from enjoying their own plans. Imagine ... skipping a port in search of *yarn!*

Save Money, Cruise More Often

Call it the Thrill Of The Hunt. I feel like I've failed when I have to pay full price for just about anything. Clothing, groceries, furniture ... part of the fun for me is knowing I paid significantly less than list price.

Cruise lines send out glossy brochures and slick email ads, but don't even think about paying those prices. Depending on depending on the specific ship, sailing date, itinerary, and much more, there are always deals to be had! Think of it as the shiny brochures car dealers pass out. Sure, the cars look great, but do you know anyone who actually pays the list price?

Internet and email newsletters are some of the best mediums for finding deals, ranging from last minute to two years out. Get a second email address if you don't want to overload your email box. Once you get in the habit of checking cruise line prices, it seems like there is always a 'sale' going on at most major cruise lines, and for good reason: there is.

Let's look at a few common "sales":

Resident Discounts: Many major cruise lines target specific states or geographic regions for a couple reasons. Far in advance of sailing, cruise lines analyze where pre-booked passengers on any given sailing live, then target ads at other areas, offering discounts to encourage booking. Closer to sailing, they might offer a sale price to Florida residents for sailings from Florida ports, or to Pacific Northwest areas on Alaska sailings. Without having to factor in air fare, people near an embarkation port can sometimes find it easier to sail, thus filling a ship to capacity. No, I still don't think this is a good enough reason to retire to south Florida!

Discounts For Third And Fourth Passengers: Look for family-friendly discounts at times when families don't normally sail. When kids are normally in school, prices for third or fourth guests in a stateroom are at their lowest and availability is at its highest. On some ships and sailings, extras in the same cabin are often steeply discounted, or even free. They don't even have to be a kid. Make sure it's someone you really like before booking four people in any cabin.

Past Guest/Loyalty Discounts: The topic of past guest discounts is well-known. A past guest's status within the cruise line loyalty program often reaps more rewards as they sail more. Free specialty dinners, beverage packages, shipboard laundry, upgrades, transfers, and lower stateroom cabins make sticking with a cruise line popular. Don't get too stuck, however, keeping in mind that other cruise lines may have a better price or itinerary to the same places.

New Cruisers: While loyalty can have its reward, cruise lines often target new cruisers, or ones who've only been on one or two voyages, with tempting prices. They constantly monitor demographics. Jumping a category by buying a new car, getting married, or passing a milestone birthday can often trigger mass mailings.

Discounted Upgrades: Closer to sailing, as cruise lines are trying to fill the ship, they may offer pre-booked passengers a discount to upgrade, or even move you to a better cabin for free. These offers are normally time-sensitive and on a first-come, first-served basis. We've lucked out several times as the Upgrade Fairy dropped by.

Specific Group Discounts: If you qualify, discounts for active or retired military members are often among the best pricing options. Firefighters, teachers, union members, and those who work in support industries like airlines, shipping, and freight company employees also might have an available discount. Watch for organization membership discounts as well, including Costco, AARP, and others. Don't hesitate to ask! Husband saved 15% one time just by being charming to the agent on the phone, then asking if they offered A Nice Guy discount.

Become familiar with the trip you've got your eye on. If you do your research, you'll get a feel for what average fares on your preferred sailing look like. When a sale or price drop comes along, you'll know it's a great deal and can act fast to snag it.

One of the best deals we've seen was $299 per person for a 14-day Panama Canal cruise on Princess, including taxes and port fees. That's far less than the port charges and canal transit fees alone! Sadly, we were in Greece that week, and had to miss out. It's the only time in my life I felt regret about going to Europe.

Move fast on deals like this—they're very limited.

Consider your booking a work in progress, rather than a line item to mark off. It's a mistake many, if not most, cruise travelers make. Fortunately, you're smarter than the average bear. Keep an eye on the prices once you're booked, checking several times a week for price drops. Even if prices drop past final payment date, you can often score an upgraded cabin or onboard credit just for the asking. If the price of the category of cabin you booked rises, pat yourself on the back and move along.

The most common method of monitoring price drops is to manually check and see if your cabin category is now selling at a lower rate. Simply do a mock booking on the cruise line's site and see if your cabin category is selling for a lower price. If it is, you can then contact the cruise line or your travel agent (whichever you booked through) to get the lower price. Online cruise-monitoring websites are easy to set up, and cost about a dollar per booking. Cheap insurance!

Simply watching for a better deal is fun, and often very profitable. On a family cruise, we saved over $800 per cabin by moving the trip back one week: same ship, same itinerary.

On one cruise, prices on similar cabins had dropped $100 per person. Being past final payment date, the cruise line was not obligated to give us anything. In this case, they upgraded our cabin from ocean view to balcony, gave us $150 in onboard credit, *and* refunded $380 in cash. That was a phone call worth making!

Other Ways to Save Money:

Be flexible, if you're able. Pricing a cruise is a lot like pricing an airline ticket; the fares go up and down constantly. Travelers who are able to **travel at the last minute** (anywhere between three to ninety days to departure) can often score the very best rock-bottom fares. You might not get your all-time favorite cabin, but you'll be on the ship, often for up to 80-90% less than the other passengers. If you can be flexible with dates, you can typically shave a few hundred dollars off your base rate. This tip works best for those who (1) can take off without much notice from their jobs, (2) are retired, or (3) live close to an embarkation port, since last minute airfares are often very pricey.

Even if you can't find a drop-dead price on a cruise, take into account proffered **cruise perks**. Free airport transfers, specialty dining, onboard credit, free beverage packages, airfare deals, free laundry services, and so on all add up. Compare, and you may find a similar sailing costs $25 more but has $400 more in onboard perks.

Of course, it only helps if they're ones you were going to use anyway. Free wine daily doesn't sway me; I don't drink wine, but if you offer free specialty restaurants or pre-paid gratuities, I'm yours. It's like the Sunday newspaper coupons at home. I don't care how great the savings is on dog food, since I have no dog.

If you use a travel agent's services to book a cruise, be sure to ask what bonuses they can throw in. Airport transfers, group discount on airfare, paid gratuities, free upgrades and specialty restaurants are common. Other add in little gifts, such as bottled water in staterooms, signed cruise books, tote bags or chocolates.

Cruise lines are in the business of filling their sailings in advance; those last-minute deals they offer are out of desperation. To that end, the pressure to book a **future cruise** while onboard your current one is intense. Along with greatly reduced deposits, you can take advantage of fare discounts and usually score free onboard credit for the current cruise or the next one. We booked a Panama Canal cruise while on a trans-Atlantic, and racked up nearly $650 in onboard credit! I'm not sure how my frugal soul will even spend that much, but it'll be fun trying.

Deposits are typically refundable, and you can choose or change itineraries in the future and even transfer your booking to your favorite travel agent to take advantage of their expertise and promotional offers. You don't even have to commit to a particular cruise on the spot; if you do, you can change it all over the place. Think of future-cruise deals like a bookmark, holding your place from one to four years, depending on the cruise line, before it actually needs to be applied towards a particular sailing.

Find out if your cruise line offers benefits for signing up for its **credit card**. With some cards you earn points that you can redeem when booking cruises, resort nights, and flights.

Book **repositioning cruises** to save money, but don't forget to add in the cost of the one-way return airfare. Since a lot of people don't like strings of sea days (I'm one of them) or can't take two weeks off for a cruise, the demand is not as high. Cruise lines often offer great deals on these sailings. Cruise lines can afford to offer good deals on repositioning cruises, knowing more sea days result in higher onboard revenue through the casino, alcohol sales, and bingo.

If you just want to cruise, don't care where, and don't want to spend a lot, opt for a place where the number of ships is high. The Caribbean continues to be the most **popular cruise destination**, with dozens of ships sailing to the Caribbean each week. Competition to fill the ships is high, resulting in better cruise deals for the Caribbean than for anyplace else in the world. This is especially true during the winter months, when cruise ships that ply Europe and Alaska during warmer weather congregate in the Caribbean.

Cruise **close to home**, if you can. You might be surprised by the number of U.S. cities you can cruise from. Ships sail from New York, Boston, Baltimore, Seattle, San Francisco, New Orleans, Los Angeles, Galveston and Houston, among others, on a seasonal or year-round basis. And don't forget Florida, which has ships sailing from Fort Lauderdale, Miami, Tampa, and Port Canaveral. Because so many cities have cruise ports, the vast majority of folks in the United States can drive less than five hours to get to a port, no flight needed. Without the cost of airfare, your cruise to regions like the Caribbean, the Bahamas, Bermuda, Mexico, Canada and New England, and Alaska suddenly gets a little bit less expensive.

If you have to fly to the embarkation port, see if a **nearby airport** will save money. Flying to an airport an hour's drive farther can sometimes be a significant savings. Rent a car, and pocket the difference. Fort Lauderdale is often cheaper than Miami, and even has an easy shuttle between airport and cruise terminal. Leaving out of Vancouver? Try

Seattle. It can save up to $200 per person, and the $35 Amtrak trip is relaxing, through scenery you'd otherwise miss.

Flying into a hub can cost less, due to competition. We find flying to Copenhagen, Stockholm, Paris, or Frankfort costs significantly less than Venice, Barcelona, or Florence, and if we take IcelandAir, it includes a layover in Iceland, up to seven days, for free!

Last year, we needed to be in Venice, but found flights were very pricy. We compared flying into other European cities. By flying into Stockholm three days early, we saved enough for a lovely weekend in a 5-star hotel, with enough left over for private tours and meals, then spent under $100 (for both of us) to fly from Stockholm to Italy. Awfully pleasant way to start a cruise.

Try to book your cruise during "**wave season**," between January and March, if you know your schedule. That's when cruise lines showcase their most aggressive offers for the year to come. The cruises can embark any time during the year, but require booking during this three-month period to catch the lower price.

Make a list of your talents. If you can find a way to **work on a cruise ship**, you'll save the entire fare, taxes, port fees and all. You may not be interested in being full-time crew member – their hours are killer – but are you a decent standup comic, a master clown, can you lecture on your interesting career or hobby? Remember, it takes 6 years to earn a PhD; if you've been obsessing over that topic for the past twenty years, you'll leave "experts" in the dust.

Major cruise lines provide free passage to guests qualified to lecture on board. Call the line's entertainment office to see if you have the necessary skills. If they want you, you'll get a free cruise for the price of a 45 minute lecture/class/ performance a few times during the sailing, and you're on your own the rest of the time. We've met photographers, financial planners, a barefoot violinist from New Brunswick, a Hawaiian historian, along with a Royal Canadian Mounted Police officer and his family, who'd talked the cruise line into adding some local color in the Canadian Maritimes.

If your **company** typically holds its morale weekend at a lodge, the big bosses might be open to making it a weekend cruise. Tell them cruise ships have business amenities such as free conference rooms, catering, and it just might work.

Want to try your hand at writing a novel set on a cruise ship? The IRS says you have five years to produce some sort of manuscript (finished or not, published or not, selling or not) in order for your cruise to count as "tax deductible research." Have you read my luscious novel, *Peril In Paradise,* set on a cruise in Hawaii? Oh, the sacrifices we writers make for our craft.

Activities Onboard

Once you've booked a cruise, bargain-hunting isn't over. Read the daily program, delivered to your cabin each night. Do it all, do nothing, but be informed either way. It'd be sad to miss something you'd enjoy, when it was available for free.

Do what actually matters to you, not what Everyone Else is doing. Your preferences and mine may be very different, but the point is to do some planning and thinking ahead of time so you know what you really want and spend accordingly. It's a matter of value for the dollar, not the lowest possible price. A balcony may be worth the cost to me; a spa treatment is not. Don't be a cheapskate, but there's no pleasure in squandering money, either.

Cruises are not all inclusive, and a person can rack up a significant bill at the end of the week. On one cruise, the cruise director confided the staff was marveling over the largest bill they'd ever seen. Not quite $10,000–for a *seven day* cruise! Mind you, that was above and beyond the cruise fare itself, just what they'd spend onboard. What had they been doing? Even with specialty restaurants, casino, and the spa, that's just nuts!

You can indulge in the spa, waste the afternoons playing (expensive!) bingo, set up camp in the casino, slosh your way through the entire bar drinks' menu, book the ship's most expensive shore excursions offered. In Europe, I was appalled to see private cars tours offered for $2865 per person for five hours. Our friends booked a private tour for the eight of us, saw everything we wanted to see and whatever else the local guide said we'd enjoy, and spent under $200 for the whole day, total. Interested? Pick up my *Mediterranean Cruise: with the Cruise Addict's Wife.*

You can rack up an astonishing bill to give the staff something to talk about... or enjoy a marvelous cruise without spending an extra penny. Instead of getting sloshed with drinks from the bar, sip the free iced tea or fruit punch. The buffet has soft or hard ice cream, and it's also free in the dining room. The live shows are included, and often are of surprisingly good quality. Personally, I've seen enough jugglers to last a couple of lifetimes, but I do admire the skill required to keep 47 plates in the air. Offerings range from magicians and aerialists, acrobats, comedians, Broadway-type shows, musicals, variety shows, improv groups, local culture and color, dancers. Watch for workshops and small-venue events, as well. Live music and nightly dance parties are part of the fun, and included.

You probably want to keep up with your exercise routine while onboard, but if you take fitness classes such as yoga, spinning, or Pilates, you may have to pay $10-$15 a pop; more if specialized equipment is involved. Instead, join the Zumba or dance classes. You can also use the ship's complimentary fitness center or hit the jogging track or promenade deck (the number of laps per mile will be conveniently marked). You don't need a regimented program to stay ship-shape; hiking in port, playing basketball onboard is just as effective at burning those double-layer-cake calories off.

Ship's photographers hover like polite mosquitoes at every gangway, often at dinner, and any time gorgeous scenery is over the rail. You can choose to pay their high fees, decide a formal portrait is just what you need, or sidestep the camera. More than likely you have a state-of-the-art HD camera sitting right there in your pocket this very instant. Why pay the ship's photographers when you can whip that thing out whenever you want? Choose your own background, and snag a passing passenger to take a few shots for you. I've never had one refuse. I smile, noticing that every single time, they take *three* shots. They're as anxious to have it turn out as you are. Often, they ask me to take theirs, next!

If you're easily sucked in by store ads, put on metaphysical blinders when you walk past the ship's shops, and also when ads are delivered to your cabin promising all sorts of deals. Be aware, though, some of the pricing, such as for on-sale bottles of alcohol or $10 clothing, is actually quite good. If you're looking for trinkets such as magnets and t-shirts, you may do better at onshore shops.

There's a reason the saying goes "The house always wins." The casino is a huge profit-generator for the cruise lines. A blackjack dealer once told me how to gamble at a casino. "Walk in, throw your money on the floor, then go gamble, recognizing that 95% of the time, you're going to lose. This way, you already lost, so you're free to enjoy the evening."

Then again, there was that one time when our friend won $5000 in two spins on a slot machine in the Mediterranean. The cruise line closed that machine for the rest of the cruise. He complained about taxes. "Here I am in the Mediterranean, on a Norwegian ship, registered in the Bahamas, and I *still* have to pay US taxes!" It's just not fair, is it?

Dancing is encouraged, whenever and wherever live music is playing, day or night. How often do you get to dance to a live band at home? At night, the disco onboard will be hoppin', and there's no cover charge!

Reading on a deck chair is a popular free activity. Bring your book, load your e-reader, visit the onboard library! I read a record eleven novels on a trans-oceanic cruise. Okay, I read pretty fast, but that was a lot, even for me. Check out books for free and return them by the last day, or peruse the free book exchange. Take a book, put yours there when you're done, saving weight as you pack, and sharing a book you've enjoyed is good karma. I see books as a river; we fish out what looks good to us, we put it back when we're done, it flows on downstream where another reader snags it. It goes on.

The ship's library/bookcase tends to be pretty picked over by the first or second day, but check back in a few days, when passengers return the books they borrowed earlier. Most libraries also have daily trivia question sheets, crossword puzzles, and Sudoku games, free for the taking.

If you're into small portable crafts, bring them along. Origami, watercolor painting, coloring books, needlework, crocheting, tying fishing flies, etc, all pass a couple of hours pleasantly on a lazy sea day. I've seen passengers crocheting or knitting on a sunny afternoon at sea, and that's great, so long as you don't inflict yourself on others; remember the sock lady.

Did you know studies show people sleep an average of ninety minutes longer on cruises than at home, and the well-rested effect can last for weeks? How often do you get to take a nap in the middle of an afternoon at home? One of my most gentle memories was of an unplanned nap on a cruise ship in Alaska. I sat in a lounge chair and nodded off, probably the result of my typical breakneck pace catching up with me. I awoke twenty minutes later, covered in a soft woolen blanket.

A crew member hurried to my chair, carrying a cup of hot split pea soup. He explained, "Madame looked chilly, so I covered you. Eat the soup; it will warm you." I don't get that kind of pampering at home!

Part of the pleasure of being at sea is *being* at sea. Gazing at the ship's wake, watching whales and flying fish or sea birds, lying on deck chairs admiring the stars costs nothing, and it's good for the soul.

On lazy sea days, you might feel like playing a game. Pack a deck of cards, or get a deck from the onboard game room. Most card room's offerings are limited, but a board game or jigsaw puzzle might pass an hour happily. Feel free to include others; you might make a new friend, which also costs nothing.

Ships also have shuffleboard, table tennis, and pool tables. Larger ships have full sports courts, mini golf, basketball, volleyball (with nets; don't worry about the ball going overboard), surf simulators, climbing walls, ropes courses, zip lines, ice skating, silly pool games, and more –all for the price of just showing up.

Ships offer complimentary group games; scavenger hunts, trivia, Pictionary, majority rules, jeopardy, or a minute-to-win-it type family game. You might see one another in a whole new light, while having a blast. I had no idea I could suck up 40 cotton balls with my nose, depositing them in a bowl, in under 30 seconds! Granted, it's not a talent I need in my daily life. Take the free juggling class offered by the magician, participate in the line dance classes, take part in the daily Zumba group. No skills needed; just show up the appointed place and time, as your daily paper details.

Look for the ship-sponsored competitions, some silly, some fierce, all free. Our son's team won the NCL Olympics. I am the proud champion of the HAL Volendam Shuffle board tournament. Okay, I beat a good-natured eleven-year-year old, but we parted friends. Bocce, putt putt golf, Wii games on a big screen, three-on-three basketball; read the daily planner to see what sounds good to you!

Watch for free cooking demonstrations, some serious, others not so much. My stomach hurt from laughing so hard at the Black Forest cake demo. I've never seen a cake leak before, and I had no idea that a frosted layer could fly farther than a Frisbee! Skills you'll never need at home are also demonstrated; napkin folding towel animals, ice sculpting, how to carve vegetable into centerpieces, origami sheep.

Many ships offer free classes on scrapbooking, jewelry making, and other crafts. They're free, and include materials. In Hawaii, the ship brought on forty thousand purple orchids and cases of kukui nuts, and taught popular classes on lei-making. We've enjoyed onboard talks on local culture and history, photography, sarong tying, writing, financial planning, all free!

Movies, both first run and older, are on the tv in your cabin, although some are pay-per-view at captive-audience prices. Many ships have cinemas, or outdoor movie screens. No need to buy tickets.

I settled on a lounge chair to watch a movie on a big screen by the pool one night. A passenger came along with a heap of pool towels before it started. She introduced herself by saying "I'm somebody's mother, and you look cold to me." Before I knew it, she had me tucked in, bundled up, and swaddled! Husband came back a minute later. Wordlessly, he pulled out his camera. Only my eyes showed. But, hey, I was snug and warm.

Ship's Time

Always pay attention to ship's time. You don't want to be Those People running down the pier as the ship sails into the sunset. It won't stop, no matter how much you wave a local clock. Ship's time rules on the high seas, and in all ports as well. You may find the ship across the pier is ahead or behind yours, and neither matches local time. Don't rely on your cell phone, which may switch to local time if you turn it on in port. Keep your watch set on ship's time, and don't ignore the onboard reminders of time zone changes. This is a silly reason to miss the ship; don't chance it!

Also, be aware of time changes on cruises. Often, as you pass through different time zones, the ship's clocks will adjust themselves, but yours needs help. Usually, you'll be notified by a card on your bed, telling you to move your own clocks ahead or behind an hour as you settle in for the night. On a recent long cruise, I was surprised to learn that the ship's time changes would be at *noon* for nine straight days. Noon is a challenging time; everyone on the ship was engaged in something at that time. Even stranger, I saw no written notification anywhere , and announcements were only made in the corridors, not in the public areas or on the TV, as most other announcements are given.

People gradually caught on as the days progressed, but for the first two or three days, passengers and staff seemed equally confused. Some were an hour late for dinner, while others complained bitterly about missing that workshop entirely. Quite a few walked around clutching the daily printed schedule, sadly asking "Does anybody know if two o'clock means two o'clock today, or two o'clock yesterday?"

If the cruise line's goal was to keep us on our toes, I must say it didn't work. Not to mention, changing one's clock one hour ahead for nine straight days was a whole lot easier that adjusting one's body that fast. I've never seen a clearer definition of "punch drunk" than the passengers on Day Fourteen.

I guess it could be worse; it could be like the Japanese Navy. No matter where they find themselves, Japanese Navy vessels are on Japan's time zone. That's not a problem when they're in the neighborhood, but when they near Greece, lunch is served promptly at three in the morning, under the glow of the moon.

....

The End

(but keep reading)

And there you have it: more cruise tips than anyone else knows about, all in one spot. If you haven't read *Cruise Tips with the Cruise Addict's Wife*, my first book, I urge you to buy it now. It's cheaper than a soda onboard, and you'll save a boatload of cash, following my tips!

Read on for Nautical Terms, and the BONUS section.

A Shameless Plea

Thanks for taking time to read More Cruise Tips---you'll be a much smarter cruiser because of it! By following my tips, you can easily save hundreds of dollars, plus you'll be one of the most-informed people on any cruise ship. Please take time to share this book with your friends. They deserve to be as smart as you, right?

I hope you'll pay me back. I would very, very, very much appreciate a 5-star review on the review page! I read every single review, and the 5 star ones absolutely make my day. Week! Five star reviews are a really big deal, like leaving a $100 tip for your cabin steward. It'll take you under three minutes to write a one-line 5 star review, and you can do it anonymously if you wish. It means a lot to me. And tell your friends!

Thanks so much!!

Nautical Terms

An easy way to insult a senior staff member is to call his beloved ship a "boat." You don't need to speak like a sailor, but at least know the difference between "left side" and "starboard."

Aft: the rear of a ship.

Amidships (pronounced 'midships'): In or toward the middle of the ship.

Astern: Behind the ship

Back-to-back: two or more cruises without much time in between. For example, a trans-Atlantic from Tampa to Barcelona, then a Barcelona to Dubai cruise leaving the same day counts as B2B cruise, even if it's on different ships.

Balcony: An exterior private seating area accessed from your cabin. Also known as a veranda.

Beam: the widest part of a ship

Bearing: position of the ship with respect to its destination; also, finding your way around the ship –often on Day Three- is called "getting your bearings"

Berth: The ship's designated parking space at the pier. Also, beds in cabins

Board: To come onto a ship.

Boat: smaller than a ship; calling a cruise ship a boat is an insult, so take care around crew and staff. Lifeboats and tenders are properly called boats.

Bow: Front of the ship.

Bridge: the navigational, command, and control center of the ship, as well as the staff who work there

Brig: an onboard 'jail' used for unruly passengers. Not all ships have a brig; some confine Bad Guys to their cabin until they can be thrown off the ship at the next port of call.

Buffet: Open-seating, carry-your-own-food casual restaurant onboard, best used for quick meals

Bulkhead: A heavy wall separating compartments on a ship

Bunker: To take on fuel. During this process, a ship's outer deck might be closed to foot traffic. Trivia: did you know the only reason cruise ships stop in Gibraltar is because it has the cheapest fuel in the world? Bunkering boats scurry around the harbor, fueling ships, while passengers go off exploring. Win, win.

Cabin: Private passenger room; also called stateroom

Captain: Master and commander of a ship. No matter the topic at hand, the Captain always has the final say-so

Comment card: Seemingly unimportant card or email questionnaire that's easily ignored, but you know better. Comment cards are used to reward or penalize crew members with money, promotions/demotions, free time, and so on. Your voice matters, so be honest, and positive!

 Cruise Director: Senior staff member who directs a staff that oversees all entertainment and passenger activities onboard, including games, classes, shows, live music

Disembark: to exit the ship, usually at the end of your cruise.

Deck: Floor of the ship, and like a hotel, the levels where parts of the ship are located. Some ships designate deck by number, others by names

Embarkation: To board a ship, or to begin a voyage.

Excursion: An organized side-trip on land, at ports of call. Excursions can be booked through the cruise line, another company, or organized on your own.

Forward: Toward the front of the ship.

Galley: Ship's kitchen, where up to 10,000 meals per day are prepared

Gang way: Ramp reaching from the pier into the side of a ship, by which passengers board. Also, a large opening in the ship's side, forming a ramp to take on supplies and provisions.

Guest Services desk: located on the main deck, often in the atrium/lobby area, this is the first stop if you have a problem, or wish to sort out your bill. Besides acting as a clearing house to direct you to the right person to help you if they can't resolve the issue themselves, Guest Services also provides trivial items you might not think about. Need a pen, pad of paper, earplugs, deck of cards, seasick meds, aspirin? Just ask.

Heading: The direction in which the ship is going, as indicated by compass points.

Hotel Director: Officer responsible for all services a land-based hotel would offer: cabins, stewards, maintenance of all public areas

Hull: The ship's outer shell. You'd worry if you knew how thin that metal is. Don't think about it.

Inside Cabin: A cabin inside the ship with no view of the water

Itinerary: Day-by-day schedule of the ship's location, including sea days and in various ports

Kids' Club: Various onboard programming provided for children, divided by age groups, usually generally consisting of games, crafts, cooking, shows, and other supervised activities in a safe play place.

Knot: Ship's speed measurement. One knot is about 15% faster than one mile per hour.

Menu: daily listing of food available in main dining room or specialty restaurants onboard. Be aware the nightly menu changes daily, so if you see a dish you'd like to try, order it now. It won't be there tomorrow. Most cruise lines offer an "always available" menu as well, offering basic foods that are offered each day of the cruise.

Main Dining Room: primary eatery on a cruise ship; formal seating with full service wait staff.

Maître d' Senior staff in dining room; person who supervises waiters and deals with passenger's issues within a dining room

Midships The middle of the ship.

Muster/ Muster Drill: Mandatory safety drill for all passengers, held within the first 24 hours of every cruise.

Attempting to skip this can have serious repercussions. Just get it over with

Ocean View Cabin/Outside Cabin: A stateroom with natural light in some form, ranging from a porthole with a partial view of the water to a large picture window.

Onboard Credit: Funds credited to your onboard charge account, often as incentive for booking this cruise through a travel agent, or booking a future cruise. Can also be compensation for a missed port or unsatisfactory issue onboard. As titled, OBC can only be spent onboard.

Pilot: Local captain brought on to advise the captain of a ship as to how to bring the ship into especially tricky ports. Pilots are not "in charge" of the ship while onboard; the only place in the world a captain relinquishes the navigation is in the Panama Canal.

Port: The left side the ship. Easy to remember because PORT and LEFT each have four letters.

Port/Port of Call: places the cruise ship stops at on the voyage. Except in a very few places where international law requires the ships to only touch land, passengers are allowed to get off the ship while in port

Porters: dockside workers who take passengers' luggage from the pier to cabins.

Porthole: A small window, usually fixed in place, not openable

Private Tour: an excursion in a port of varying length arranged by passengers on their own. Travel Agents can also set these up. Invariably, they cost less than a tour through the cruise line, you'll see and do more, and you'll have the flexibility a large, regimented tour with 65 of your new best friends lacks.

Production Crew: main entertainment troupe on the ship; headliners, singers and dancers. Does not include show band, piano players, random musicians, or one time acts, such as comics, legacy bands, or jugglers

Promenade: the outer deck encircling the ship, designed for walking, lounging and admiring the ocean. Usually on lower decks. On mega-ships, promenade refers to the shopping area onboard, or the main open walkway of the ship.

Provisions: All the food, supplies and equipment needed by a cruise ship, taken on at pre-determined ports. With regard to foodstuffs, shrimp is the most expensive commodity, so eat up.

Seating: Designated fixed dining times on ships that have set times. Most large ships have a version of open seating, too, which works pretty much like any land-based restaurant

Security: the at-sea equivalent of a police department onboard. Besides keeping order and investigating crimes, Security has the power to make your life really miserable for infractions, from fines, confinement to your cabin of the brig, up to throwing you off the ship in the next port. Behave yourself.

Shipboard Charge Account: Ships are cashless; this is the running tally of onboard expenditures

Ship-Sponsored Shore Excursion: Any in-port tour arranged through the cruise line itself. Prices tend to be higher than private tours, often they involve crowds on busses, and you'll invariably see less than you would on your own.

Stabilizer: Hydraulic activated folding underwater 'wings' extended to minimize ship's sideways motions in rough seas. Expensive to use, they're not deployed as often as seasick passengers would wish.

Starboard: The right-hand side of the ship. STARBOARD and RIGHT HAND each have nine letters, making it easy to differentiate from Port and Left, both of which have four letters

Stateroom: a private passenger cabin, also known as a cabin.

Stern: The rear point of the ship.

Steward: Person who services a cabin. May have an assistant. Often a great source of information, and the person to ask first if you need anything, such as a fatter pillow, a child-size life vest, more ice, etc.

Suite: A larger cabin with "more." "More" can be space, a balcony, or amenities

Trans- Atlantic or Trans-Pacific cruise: one way lengthy cruises itineraries, usually repositioning to new areas for the season. TAs can be surprisingly inexpensive, but don't forget to factor in the one-way return airfare.

Travel Agent: Person or agency skilled in booking cruises and other forms of travel. Beware: they're paid by the cruise line, airline, hotel, etc, so don't let them suck you into paying booking fees! Some even charge for phone calls. From these unscrupulous agents, run.

Tender: A boat used to transfer passengers from the ship to the shore and back again when the ship is anchored offshore in ports without sufficient pier space. Often these are the ship's own lifeboats; we've also experienced a rental Greek fishing boat off Greece that smelled like ...a Greek fishing boat

Tender Tickets: System used to determine in what order passengers may exit a ship via a tender. Priority is given to VIP guests, then those who booked tours through the cruise line, then the Everybody Elses.

Travel Insurance: Pre-purchased insurance that reimburses in case of illness, emergency evacuation, or a variety of other conditions which might interrupt your cruise. Coverage varies widely, as does price

Upper Berth: A Pullman-style bunkbed recessed into a cabin's wall or ceiling, lowered by cabin stewards at night to accommodate extra passengers, and folded up out of the way during the daytime

Waiter: Person who services a table during meals, usually with an assistant. Waiters work meal times only, thus allowing more time on shore in ports, making them a good resource for advice in port

Wake: The churned-up waves left behind a ship as it moves through the water, best viewed from the aft of the ship. Need to lose your troubles? Staring at the wake helps, every time!

Weigh Anchor: To raise the anchor, a noisy event signaling more adventures ahead

BONUS:

Excerpt from _Mediterranean Cruise With The Cruise Addict's Wife_

Provisions

On one of the days-at-sea, Husband and I took a behind the scenes ship tour. Fascinating! I like food, and I'm pretty knowledgeable about it. Not as good as my son, who can write a recipe for a dish after tasting it once, but I do like the stuff. The _Spirit_ has eleven restaurants, plus eight bars and lounges, all serviced by the same storage and prep areas. Several have their own kitchens for last –minute food preparation, but the preliminary prep all takes place in the bowels of the ship.

The food storage takes place on different decks, depending on whether or not the food is considered to be clean or dirty. "Clean" food is packaged and dry goods, raw meats and seafood, and also prepared foods such as peeled onions and chopped carrots. "Dirty" is any food requiring further prep before cooking, like baking potatoes still in the box that need scrubbing, carrots that need to be peeled, onions waiting to be peeled and chopped, and meats or fish that have not yet been butchered into serving portions. Peelings and dirt and leaves and trimmings never make it to the main galley; only ready-to-cook foods are delivered to the chefs and cook staff, by people pushing carts at breakneck speed, using the designated elevators. Separate "Clean" and "Dirty" _elevators_---wow!

Including crew, staff, and the passengers, an average of 10,000 meals per day are served on the Spirit. And you complain about making dinner couple nights a week!

I was impressed with how close to the mark the ordering of provisions manages to be. There is very little waste---how do they possibly predict that? I don't do that well in my grocery shopping at home, and there are a whole lot less people at my dinner table!

The Provisions Officer explained to us that the order he makes ahead of time varies, considerably, by the passengers. It's made one month in advance. The Captain is provided with a passenger list with ages, nationalities, and, of course, the number of passengers on board; a full cruise ship obviously requires many more provisions than a less-full sailing. The Captain gives the list to the Provisions Officer, the Provisions Officer consults with the Executive Chef, then makes an order, okayed last minute by the Captain. Captains are in charge of everything, even overseeing details like how many eggs are ordered.

The provisions order is influenced by many criteria, including the time of year, age of passengers, their nationalities, and even the expected weather on the cruise itinerary. Orders for the buffet and the grills on board vary much more the main dining rooms or specialty restaurants, which are fairly steady. If there are a lot of kids on the cruise, say, during summer and holiday vacations, they lay in more french fries, pizza, chicken tenders, and a whole lot more ice cream. If there's an older clientele, such as on a longer itinerary, they order in more fruit and sweets, especially prunes and dessert ingredients. For some reason, older people crave sweets. And prunes; don't think about it.

If the population has a large European contingent, the cruise line orders more wine, chocolate desserts, and extra red meats, such as lamb and duck. On more casual itineraries, such as in the Caribbean, or when there are a lot of American passengers on board, they make sure to have extra burgers, hotdogs, a whole lot of coffee, craft beers, extra beef, chicken, and less of upscale things such as caviar and escargot. When a lot of Germans are on board, extra pork and bacon are ordered; not so when Israelis make up a significant part of the passenger list. This isn't exactly racial profiling; certainly, categorizing by age and nationality, though! It'd be easier to argue, if they weren't so amazingly accurate.

Holidays and time of year also affect the provisions required onboard. More cookies in December, more prepackaged kosher meals over Jewish holy days, more fresh fruit during summer months. When you think about it, it's probably the same though process you use to make up your own grocery list---only on a much larger scale!

If the ship is going somewhere colder, such as Scandinavia, or perhaps Alaska, they lay in extra coffee, hot cocoa mixes, and they plan on going through a lot of soup. If the passenger list includes a lot of Asian nationals, plan on extra rice noodles and fish, plus extra rice ---although the crew alone goes through 400 lbs of rice per week!

On cruises with a lot of high- priced suites booked, and elite cruisers, VIPs, or upper-level loyalty members, the Provisions Officer plans on additional large strawberries for those daily big juicy chocolate covered strawberries in the cabins, along with extra fancy items such as prosciutto, cheeses, caviar, champagne, large shrimp, extra lobster, more chocolates, and high-end meats.

Think about cheese. Plain old American cheese is the best for melting on a burger, but not suitable for a fancy cheese tray at an Owner's Suite party. Someone had to plan that, and that is just one item!

Besides nationality and climate, the cruise line also factors in quality. For example, when we were on the Spirit, I personally noticed at least four sizes of shrimp. There was salad size in the buffet salads, and medium-size shrimp appeared on the surf and turf in the main dining room. In the specialty restaurants, the shrimp cocktail had a larger size. The biggest one I saw were offered as hors d'oeuvres at the Captain's VIP cocktail party. That's a lot of variety, and it's only *shrimp!* Meats, such as steak, also come in varying quality and size, and must be ordered according. For example, in the main dining rooms a plain strip steak is on the menu. In the steakhouse on the Spirit, a 16 ounce rib eye was on the menu. Depending on the demographics of the ship that particular cruise, they may anticipate a run on the steak house, or the buffet may be more popular. All of this changes the provisions order.

I wanted to know where the ship's provisions came from on this particular itinerary. We noticed that, for example, that the milk and other dairy products were different than in any other cruise ship we had been on before, although we still saw very familiar items as well. I was told that they provision in Venice and again in Citivecchia, which is Rome's port. Ten containers come from the USA, sealed shipping containers, the size that goes on the back of a semi-truck. TEN of them--- for only one cruise! Those are referred to a 'heavy store' and it includes dry provisions and canned items. All the frozen meat and fish also come from North America; from Miami, in this case. That vision you have of the chef plying a fishing pole over the aft deck catching your dinner isn't based on reality, but it does sound fun!

On this cruise, the ship takes on fresh foods, including fruits and vegetables, non-frozen meats, and all dairy, in Venice and again in Citivecchia (Rome's port). That's why, for breakfast, we could find Kellogg's Frosted Flakes, but the milk was a little different than we were used to ... kind of thick, kind of almost –yogurt flavor and texture. We didn't like the milk. Personal preference!

Ten minutes after the ship makes port on Embarkation Day, the ship's Provisions Officer and his staff are already busy with their clipboards, checking every pallet and crate of food as it is delivered to the ship. Besides keeping a fanatically accurate count, they check for any spoiled fruit and vegetables. Each pallet is then directed to the proper area, to be stored at a specific temperature. Red wine goes into a warmer room than white wine, beer, and champagne, for example. Blueberries never share space with flour.

We walked through the provisions rooms on the behind the scenes tour, including the dry storage, freezers, refrigerators, proofing rooms, thawing chambers; pretty much all over. I recognized many of the brands and was impressed with the quality of the NCL purchases. The provisions are stored floor-to-ceiling in the beginning of the cruise. Towards the end of every cruise, it gets down to nothing much at all; just a day or two of foodstuffs remain. The ship always has extra ice cream and meats onboard; being frozen, those items have a much longer shelf life than, say, fresh berries. This ship had enough ice cream alone to fuel a couple of elementary schools!

The Provisions officer explained that they plan for the length of the cruise, plus two days, to account for delays, such as port problems or weather issues. If the ship is unable to make the disembarkation port for any reason, throwing together another meal or two is taken in stride. Good planning—if they were to run out of food, there could be a mutiny onboard! We've heard horror stories about the Carnival ship that ran out of food and was not able to return to port, about how people survived on crackers and Spam and mayonnaise sandwiches. That kind of story is bad PR, among other things.

All food categories are stored separately; the fish never meets the flour, the fruit never shares a room with the chicken. Every bin, bowl, cart, or bag is carefully covered with clear plastic wrap to protect it. There are different lockers for different meats; red meat, poultry and fish all have their own refrigerators for thawing and freezers for storing.

Food Prep

There are five butchers on board the *Spirit*. Just five! They break down the larger meats into serving portions. At the time we were there, one butcher was frenching a mountain of lamb chops for the dining room menu the following night. I thought five butchers was an awfully small number for the whole ship, until I saw this guy's speed! His knife moved so fast it was blurry. It looked extremely sharp and I was pleased to see that he had a metal chain mail glove on his other hand.

We learned that there are three sub-cooks in charge of produce preparation. For example, if the chef requires chopped onions, he does not chop his own onion. The chefs must order what they need for the following day; say, ten pounds of diced onions. Down in the bowels of the ship, one of the produce workers will peel and chop a sufficient amount of onions-- only ten pounds was a lot less than the real number! By the time the chef reaches for them, those onions have been cleaned, peeled, chopped, weighed, and wrapped in plastic. While we were there, we talked to one of the crew, who was peeling carrots. He said that that he would peel and dice 200 pounds before the day was over. Carrot soup on the menu? The kitchen crew works twelve hours a day, yet still had warm smiles for us interlopers. Imagine spending twelve hours peeling onions and putting carrots through the dicer, knowing the sacks of cabbage have your name on them next?

Norwegian Cruise Line has the best bread on the open sea, in my opinion. I especially enjoy NCL's croissants and pretzel rolls. All bread, including rolls, specialty breads, croissants, hot dog buns, sandwich bread, those yummy pretzel rolls, and all desserts are all made on board from scratch. This saves space in storage. Of course the bread products are fresher and they tend to be tastier than packaged items. On a personal level, it's kind of a nice thought to think of people making bread in the middle of the night so that I can have fresh challah for my French toast for breakfast. I hope they take a nap later on.

In the bakery, I admired the state-of-the-art equipment; sheet rollers, dough rounders, proofing racks, glass fronted ovens leaking enticing aromas. Two crew members were very busy making the multigrain rolls for dinner that night, weighing out individual portions on a scale. I'm not sure the weight of all that dough, but I know I could not have contained it on my kitchen table. It may not have fit in my grandchild's swimming pool, either. And that was only one product.

The quantities were overwhelming! We saw trays and trays of cookies, cakes, and beautiful desserts, all lined up, ready and waiting for the night's dinner service. Whole turkeys were roasting in the ovens, pans of braising lamb shank, along with vats of soup and heaps of fresh vegetables waiting their turns. Baked pastries and breads cooled on tall racks, while unbaked items slowly rotated in the proofing area. The Cruise Addict made a new friend—not sure how, but Husband ended up with a warm cookie!

Cleanliness is taken very seriously by Norwegian Cruise Line. Cruise ships are very sensitive to illness outbreaks in any form, and they go to pretty extreme lengths to avoid the food-borne variety. Sanitation is about as good as your local clinic. There are two elevators for dish transportation; dirty dishes have their own elevator, while clean items never cross their paths. We noticed that the clean utensils all had plastic wrap on them, from hotel pans down to the smallest whisks and ladles. No one has to ask, "Hey, is this clean or dirty?" as we do at home. It's a good idea, but not one I'm likely to adopt.

The preparation areas in the galley looked immaculate to me, but being nosy, I took time to step aside and peek into a floor drain. I figured if there's any gunk or dirt, that's where it's going to be. I happily report that the tile floor drain was pristine and white, as clean as a countertop. Not clean enough to eat off of; it was still a floor drain, after all, but you get the idea.

A Shopping List

The Provisions Officer gave us this list of stores onboard for a seven day cruise:

24,236 pounds of beef

5,040 pounds of lamb

7,216 pounds of pork

4,600 pounds of veal

1,680 pounds of breakfast sausage

10,211 pounds of chicken

3,156 pounds of turkey

13,851 pounds of fish

350 pounds of shelled crab

2,100 pounds of lobster

25,736 pounds of fresh vegetables

15,150 pounds of potatoes

1800 pounds of butter

20,003 pounds of fresh fruit and berries

3,260 US gallons of milk

1,976 US quarts of heavy cream

600 US gallons of ice cream

9,235 dozen eggs

5,750 pounds of sugar

2,500 lbs butter

2,600 lbs cheeses

2,000 lbs sugar

3,800 pounds of rice

1,750 pounds of cereal

450 pounds of jelly and jam

2,458 pounds of coffee

2,450 tea bags

120 pounds of herbs and spices, both dry and fresh

3,100 dozen eggs

3,400 bottles of assorted wines

2000 bottles of champagne

2000 bottles of gin

290 bottles of vodka

350 bottles of whiskey

150 bottles of rum

45 bottles of sherry

600 bottles of assorted liqueurs

10,100 bottles/cans of beer

... and the list goes on!

....

Please remember to leave a review. They mean more than you know!

other books by DEB GRAHAM:

<u>Tips From The Cruise Addict's Wife</u>

<u>Mediterranean Cruise with the Cruise Addict's Wife</u>

<u>Peril In Paradise</u>   a cruise novel

<u>How To Complain ...and get what you deserve</u>

<u>How To Write Your Story In 30 Minutes a Day</u>

<u>Hungry Kids Campfire Cookbook</u>

<u>Quick and Clever Kids' Crafts</u>

<u>Kid Food On A Stick</u>

<u>Awesome Science Experiments for Kids</u>

<u>Savory Mug Cooking</u>

<u>Uncommon Household Tips</u>

Made in the USA
Middletown, DE
15 June 2017